About *Falling in Love... Finding God*

The theme and substance of Falling in Love... Finding God is the integration of our marital journey to union with each other and our spiritual journey to union with God. Specifically, we integrate the Four Weeks of the Spiritual Exercises with the four Stages of marital growth and show that the spiritual journey of the Exercises is the same as the journey of married love. Reading the book and doing and sharing the reflection questions will lead couples to recognize that they are living holy lives of love and intimacy and inspire them to desire even deeper intimacy.

Using the insights and stories from our 40+ years of our journey, we lead couples to find love, intimacy, and God in their experiences. Along the way, we offer practical marriage tools such as communication and conflict resolution as well Ignatian spirituality tools such as Discernment and Examen. This book also offers encouragement for couple to reach out to others (mission).

And with the grace of the Holy Spirit, we hope that our readers will know and experience the following:

- how the conscious living of marriage and spirituality can reveal God in our daily, ordinary lives, and impact everything that we do;
- how the blending of head and heart can allow us to live our marriage with joy, depth, and authenticity;
- how using Scripture leads us to discover how the Word of God speaks to us as married couples;
- how to use prayer and meditation guided by the Spiritual Exercises of St. Ignatius;
- how the discernment process will lead to mutually desirable choices and give us the energy and freedom to implement the discernment;
- how marriage expands our world view;
- how to live an integrated whole life rather than juggling separate spiritual, marriage, family, work, and individual lives.

Endorsements

Tim and Sue Muldoon

Jerome L. Shen and M. Bridget Brennan have done a great service: inviting those who are married or to-be-married to an experience of Saint Ignatius Loyola's Spiritual Exercises. Those who have been married a long time understand how the relationship with a spouse is the primary experience of vocational life, and as such it is the primary lens through which we come to understand the sacramental presence of God. Shen and Brennan call us to reflect on that vocation, drawing on their many years of ministry to the married and their deep knowledge of the Spiritual Exercises. We warmly recommend this book both to those who have seen many seasons of married life, and to those yet to embark on this beautiful vocation. Let them be your guides to an experience of the living God, through a reflective pilgrimage in the company of your beloved.

Tim and Sue Muldoon, authors of *Six Sacred Rules for Familie, The Discerning Parent: An Ignatian Guide to Raising Your Teenager,* and other books.

Dr. Ann M. Garrido

I have known Jerry and Bridget now for close to twenty years, as we both share a common Jesuit parish home. In addition to their professional careers and parenting two remarkable sons, they have always dedicated a significant portion of their time to lifting up the sacrament of marriage in our church—through their writing and speaking, their leadership in pre-engagement counseling and marriage preparation, and marriage enrichment programs. They are a constant witness to the power of the sacrament to heal and bridge and grow not only persons but our wider world.

In this book, they propose to highlight the particular link that they have discovered between the stages of married life and the Ignatian exercises—a link, which to my knowledge, has not been made before in such an explicit way. The reflection and discussion questions they offer can help other couples to also discover the power of an Ignatian framework for developing in their own marriages.

One of the things I appreciate most in Bridget and Jerry's writing is their vulnerability. Their stories illumine the multiple, daily ways in which we have a choice to turn toward or away from one another. And they show how discernment is just as much a part of the marital vocation as it is a priestly or religious vocation. Bridget and Jerry are pioneers in exploring what Ignatian spirituality looks like when embraced wholeheartedly in the lay life.

Dr. Ann M. Garrido, Associate Professor, Aquinas Institute of Theology, Author, *Redeeming Administration* (2013) and *Redeeming Conflict* (2016)

James Martin, SJ

It is surprising that so little has been written on marriage from the Ignatian point of view. Surprising because Ignatius's inviting and accessible spirituality, which speaks of how to love freely, how to center oneself in Christ and how to make good decisions, is a natural fit for couples longing to lead loving lives. In their new book, this husband and wife team provide a wonderful introduction for how to incorporate Ignatian spirituality into the married life. In doing so they have done a great service to married couples, and, therefore, to the church.

James Martin, SJ, author of *The Jesuit Guide to (Almost) Everything; Jesus: A Pilgrimage; Becoming Who you are* and many other books.

John Padberg, S.J.

Here is an insightful, imaginative, personal and practical book with a high ambition that it succeeds in fulfilling.

The husband and wife co-authors want to describe their twofold growth in intimacy with God and with each other in their marriage as a help toward such a growth in other married couples. They do so in the context of an imaginative and persuasive correspondence of the "weeks" or stages of the Ignatian *Spiritual Exercises* and the stages of the growth of a loving intimacy in marriage. As they say, "We are an ordinary couple living our commitments to marriage and to our faith as best we can . . . . through forty years of marriage." Many other couples will find moving and persuasive their writing on "the integration of the spiritual and marital life" from bliss and enchantment through dissatisfaction and frustration to honesty and courage to a love of God and of each other that is made ever more transforming through each other.

And lest prospective readers be put off by what at first sight might seem an impossibly high ideal, they are brought down to earth by practical examples and stories of such a marriage lived day by day. Read this book slowly, wife and husband; it will grow on you as does the love of each other and of God toward which it leads you.

John Padberg, S.J., internationally recognized scholar and author, former Director of the Institute for Jesuit Sources

William Barry, SJ

Bridget Brennan and Jerome Shen have written a fine and helpful book on the interplay of intimacy with God and intimacy in marriage. Using their own experience of growing in intimacy with God and with one another through Ignatian spirituality, they offer to take couples through the stages of growth in both intimacies. At the end of each chapter the authors give couples very helpful exercises that they can do separately and together. If you use this book, you will find that you are growing together as a couple while, at the same time, growing closer to God. Since closeness to God and to one another never stops there, the effects brighten the world around you.

William A. Barry, S.J., author of *Finding God in All Things*; *Paying Attention to God*; *God's Passionate Desire and Our Response* and many other books.

Michael V. Tueth, S.J.

The happily married Jerome Shen and M. Bridget Brennan remind us that St. Ignatius Loyola began composing the Spiritual Exercises while he was still a layman. While we often associate the work with Jesuits and other consecrated religious, Jerry and Bridget demonstrate how the Spiritual Exercises are a guide for married couples to achieve greater intimacy and holiness by finding God in their daily graces and challenges. While they shape their book on the pattern of the four weeks of the Exercises, they also illustrate how they have experienced the working of Ignatian spirituality with their own personal stories and their work with married couples over the years. Amid the huge number of books on Ignatian spirituality and on marriage counseling, this book in its own unique way blends the two issues in a most convincing and helpful way.

Michael V. Tueth, S.J., Professor Emeritus, Fordham University

FALLING IN LOVE
... FINDING GOD

Marriage and the
Spiritual Exercises of
St. Ignatius of Loyola

Donna + John
May your love for
one another lead you
to know God's love —

Bridget Brennan +
Jerry Shen

M. Bridget Brennan and Jerome L. Shen

ISBN: 978-1-4834-7036-8 (sc)
ISBN: 978-1-4834-7037-5 (e)

Library of Congress Control Number: 2017908044

Lulu Publishing Services rev. date: 6/5/2017

We dedicate this book to

Pope Francis,

Champion of marriage and family

"The Joy of Love experienced by families is also the joy of the Church."

"Each marriage is a kind of 'salvation history', which from fragile beginnings – thanks to God's gift and a creative and generous response on our part – grows over time into something precious and enduring. Might we say that the greatest mission of two people in love is to help one another become, respectively more a man and more a woman. Fostering Growth means helping a person to shape his or her own identity." (Amoris Laetitia)

Contents

Acknowledgements

This book is the result of a long journey of faith and relationships that goes back to the 1600s when the Shen family in Shanghai, Jerry's birthplace, was converted to Christianity by French Jesuit missionaries. Many generations later, the Ignatian charism continues to thrive and animates our marriage today. In fact, it was there from the beginning. The two of us met in the John XXIII Christian Life Community (CLC), part of a lay movement grounded in the Spiritual Exercises of St. Ignatius. We both participated actively at the local, national, and international levels.

In addition to the love and support we received from our local CLC, we were nourished as individuals, as a couple, as family by the many opportunities that the national and world CLC federations provided. Our now-adult sons look back on and recall fondly the adventures of attending the CLC conventions and conferences throughout the United States.

It would be challenging to name all the people who have touched our lives and who have contributed in some way to this book. Our parents, people of deep and unwavering faith, passed on to us the gift of faith in our childhood. Indeed, that deep faith is the strongest bond between us, who are from different races and different economic strata, and who have different last names and very different personalities.

The most significant person on our Ignatian marriage journey was a Jesuit priest, Father Tom Curry, who guided our discernment to marriage. He knew in his heart that we would be called to marriage ministry in some way. He planted the seed that led us to participate in Ignatian retreats and to receive spiritual direction as a couple. It was on our journey with Tom that we first experienced a love relationship that mirrors the Trinity. Since that time, many others have befriended, guided, and supported us along the way.

We also thank the following people who reviewed our manuscript and offered valuable suggestions: Michael Harter, SJ; Marian Cowan, CSJ; (†) Rosemary Jermann; Deb Meister; Francis Nichols; Sara and Kevin Lee; Lucien Roy; Gene Donahue,SJ; Jean Monahan; Kathy McGrath, RSCJ; and Michael Tueth, SJ. A special thank you to Mary Domahidy, Professor Emerita, St. Louis University for creating the Love Everlasting symbol.

We are grateful for those who took time to read and endorse our book: William Barry, SJ; Ann Garrido, James Martin, SJ; Tim and Sue Muldoon; John Padberg, SJ; and Michael Tueth, SJ.

Additionally, we wish to thank the following friends and colleagues for their affirmation and assistance in sharing, suggesting, and connecting us with resources: Ron Mercier, SJ, Provincial UCS; Dan White, SJ, Pastor of St. Francis Xavier (College) Church; Tim Godfrey, SJ; Len Kraus, SJ; J.J. Mueller, SJ; Michael Tueth, SJ; Robert O'Toole, SJ; Joe and Mary Milner; Lisa Reiter; and Marie Schimelfening. A special thanks to our faithful prayer supporter, Alice Weis. Her prayers kept us moving forward. We are in gratitude for the witness of CLC communities. The seeds for this book were planted in Christian Life Community. We thank the community at St. Francis Xavier (College) Church who nourished us and the Ignatian Volunteer Corps, whose members' lives validate this book.

> **May all that we do, all that we are, and all that we are invited to be, lead us to a deeper realization and union with the Trinity dwelling within us. May we always be grateful to all those who touch our lives with their love.**

AMDG

Bridget and Jerry

I
Introduction

Fall in Love

Nothing is more practical than
finding God, that is than falling in love,
in a quite absolute, final way.
What you are in love with,
what seizes your imagination, will affect everything.
It will decide
what will get you out of bed in the morning,
what you do with your evenings,
how you spend your weekends,
what you read, whom you know,
what breaks your heart,
and what amazes you with joy and gratitude.
Fall in Love, stay in love,
and it will decide everything.

From *Finding God in All Things: A Marquette Prayer Book* © 2009 Marquette University Press. Used with permission.

Attributed to Fr. Pedro Arrupe, SJ. *Father Arrupe, the 28th Superior General of the Jesuits, was loved by many. He died in 1991 after a long post-stroke illness.*

> **The integration of our spiritual journey to union with God and our marital journey to union with each other constitutes the theme and substance of this book.**

We have found that these journeys are not only concurrent but are one and the same journey to deeper love, intimacy, and union. Growing in intimacy with God inspires us to greater love and intimacy with each other. Loving each other leads us to greater gratitude for God's love. The integration of these two journeys of love has brought us peace, gratitude, and joy and has affected every aspect of our daily lives. Love and joy give us motivation to seek the ideal. Paraphrasing Father Arrupe,

Love gets us out of bed in the morning and gives us energy for the day.

Love decides what we do with our evenings and weekends.

Love energizes us to reach out to others.

Love guides us on what decisions we make.

Love tells us how to raise our children and relate to our relatives.

Love affects how we earn and spend our money.

Love sensitizes us to what breaks our hearts and what amazes us with joy and gratitude.

Benefits for Readers

We are an ordinary couple living our commitments to marriage and to our faith as best as we can. Through the many years of marriage, we have received many blessings from these commitments. In the words of Pope Francis, "For if we have received the love which restores meaning to our lives, how can we fail to share that love with others?"[1] In sharing our learnings and our blessings, we hope to inspire and guide our readers to experience and cherish the many blessings of their own spiritual and marital journeys. And with the grace of the Holy Spirit, we hope that our readers will know and experience the following:

- how the conscious living of marriage and spirituality can reveal God in our daily, ordinary lives, and impact everything that we do;

---

[1] Pope Francis. *The Joy of the Gospel Evangelii Gaudium* (Nov 24, 2013), No 8 (Washington, DC: USCCB)

- how the blending of head and heart can allow us to live our marriage with joy, depth, and authenticity;
- how a stable, faith-filled marriage provides a firm foundation for children;
- how using Scripture leads us to discover how the Word of God speaks to us as married couples;
- how to use prayer and meditation guided by the Spiritual Exercises of St. Ignatius;
- how the discernment process will lead to mutually desirable choices and give us the energy and freedom to implement the discernment;
- how marriage expands our world view;
- how our love for one another moves us out of ourselves to be a "people for others;"
- how to live an integrated whole life rather than juggling separate spiritual, marriage, family, work, and individual lives.

Ideals and Motivations Forged in the Furnace of Real Encounters

In the above, we have expressed our motivations for living our lives and the ideals we hope to achieve in our life. These ideals and motivations spring from God's call and our mutual love for each other. In living our lives now, these ideals are being refined and forged in the furnace of real encounters with the outside world. Our soul awakened by the Holy Spirit desires to love God, to love others, and to do good works. But as we try to carry out those desires, we face obstacles in ourselves, in others that we try to love, and in the real physical world outside of ourselves. And as we work through those roadblocks to love, we come to greater understanding of God's ideal for us in our real circumstances and gain greater freedom to do what we are called to do.

About Us

Jerry's Story

(**Jerry**) I was born in Shanghai, China and was given a Christian name of Jerome because my birthday was close to the feast day of St. Jerome. I was baptized and confirmed in the French Jesuit Cathedral of Shanghai. In 1949, my father returned from his medical residency in St. Louis, to bring my mother, my sister, and myself out of Shanghai to St. Louis. We were very lucky to leave one week after the Communist army occupied Shanghai.

In St. Louis, I attended Catholic grade schools, a Jesuit high school and Jesuit Saint Louis University. I have a doctor of philosophy degree in chemistry from the University of Wisconsin. I am a high introvert on the Myers-Briggs scale, and I am hesitant to meet new people. I concentrated on my studies in part to compensate for my poor social skills.

My spiritual formation was in the atmosphere of the 1950 St. Louis Catholic Church. I was taught that our goal in life is to reach heaven and that following the rules of the Church will get us there. As the first born in my family, I was very responsible and took my obligations very seriously. There was daily mass at school and regular weekly confessions. In high school, I made yearly Ignatian retreats. At Saint Louis University, I joined the Sodality, which later evolved into the Christian Life Community (CLC) and continue to do retreats every year. After graduate school, I joined John XXIII CLC in St. Louis, where I met and fell in love with Bridget.

These choices for spiritual growth were freely made and I enjoyed them, even my childhood experiences. I enjoyed being in the pre- and post-Vatican II Church and experiencing the transition.

I started dating Bridget in 1973. It was at a CLC retreat while contemplating a passage from St. Paul (Ephesians 3:14–19) that I realized I loved her. We made our discernment for marriage with our dear friend, Jesuit priest Tom Curry, while on a private retreat as a couple. And ever since, we have tried to grow together in our spirituality and in our relationship.

Looking back, I can sense the continual presence of God guiding and inspiring me and us. How else can I explain my escape from Shanghai, the continual Ignatian formation, and a shy Chinese immigrant boy from a wealthy family who had maids and an Irish-American girl from a working-class family, whose great aunts were maids, falling and growing in love for over 40-plus years?

Bridget's Story

(**Bridget**) So following Jerry's introduction, I would be that Irish-American girl from a working-class family. In terms of church and school, I had a similar experience to Jerry's: attended Catholic grade school, high school and college. I was very close to my family and spent much time with my parents, siblings, and my many nieces and nephews. I also enjoyed my work as an elementary school teacher.

A year after Jerry and I were married, I gave birth to our first child. During the pregnancy, Jerry and I had discerned that I would stay home with our son. Two years later, our second son was born. I remained at home as a stay-at-home Mom for about 10 years.

I then had the opportunity to become a pastoral minister at our parish, St. Francis Xavier, where I developed a family faith formation program, a youth ministry program, and parish life ministry. I loved my ministry and our Pastor. Father Len Kraus, SJ, was wonderfully supportive to staff. I could coordinate my work hours per our sons' school schedule. It was the best of both worlds.

Some years later as our sons went off to college, I established the Cana Institute, where I have developed a marriage preparation program, retreats for couples and workshops for singles. I am a trained marriage and relationship coach as well as a spiritual director and facilitator guide for small faith groups.

My passion is sharing the good news that married people live very holy lives in their day-in and day-out fidelity to one another and to the Church.

Introduction to the Spiritual Exercises of St. Ignatius of Loyola

The Spiritual Exercises grew out Ignatius of Loyola's personal experience as a man seeking to grow in union with God and to discern God's call. While recovering from a battle wound, he had conversion experiences. He remembered and reflected on how these experiences affected his intellectual, emotional, psychological, and spiritual being. He shared and compared experiences with his companions. Although all encounters with God are unique, he found common themes and patterns. He could discern what experiences led to God and what experiences did not lead to God. He recognized that there is a logical psychological and spiritual sequence to growing in love with God. Wanting others, especially his companions to continually experience God's love, he developed the "Spiritual Exercises."

Rather than a description of his experiences and learnings, St. Ignatius created an instrument of prayers, reflections, and guidance that can lead us to a personal, firsthand encounter with God. He is like a playwright who evokes emotional reactions from the audience through the actions on the stage. The Spiritual Exercises can be viewed as a play in four acts that draws us closer to God. In this way, the Spiritual Exercises never get old, for they can be repeated over and over again with old or new audiences. Each time we do it, we encounter God anew.

The Four Weeks of the Spiritual Exercises

The Spiritual Exercises are organized according to a logical, psychological and spiritual sequence of growing in love and relationship as follows:

First, before we can enter relationship, we must accept that we are lovable and desire to love in return. Fear that we are not lovable can keep us from relationships. An experience of love will reduce our fear and awaken our desire to love.

Second, once we are desirous of loving, we must seek a lover (God) and make a mutual commitment to remain in relationship.

Third, we must live out the commitment carrying our crosses and cherishing the joys.

Finally, we enter the perfection of relationship. We are in total union with God.

The Spiritual Exercises are organized in the above dynamic movements as Four Weeks. The Four Weeks indicate stages of spiritual growth and do not signify a span of time. St. Ignatius advises the retreatant to stay in the dynamic of a given week until the purpose and the growth desired for the Week is achieved.

First Week

We believe the purpose of the first week of prayers and reflections is to bring about an experience of God's love for us. For this experience will free us from our fears and inspire a desire to love God.

The First Week of the Exercises is a time of reflection on our lives in the light of God's boundless love for us. The first week starts with a discussion of what we are called to do and how we are to respond to God's love — The Principle and Foundation.

After that, we reflect on our personal and corporate sins and their consequences. We look at God's response of love and God's desire to forgive and reconnect with us. Seeing the history of God's love for us even when we sin brings a new experience of God's love. And in the power of that love, we gain the courage to free ourselves from our fears that cause sin and acquire the strength to love.

Second Week

In the Second Week, we look for Jesus as someone we want to love. The meditations and prayers of the second week teach us to follow Christ as his disciples. We reflect on the Scripture passages on Jesus' life and ministry. Through our loving encounters with Jesus, we are moved to make decisions to love him more intimately and to do his work in the world. The goal of the second week is to make an unconditional commitment to love and serve God.

Third Week

The purpose of the Third Week is to gain strength to live out our commitment to love and serve God. We meditate on Christ's Last Supper, passion, and death. We see his suffering and the gift of the Eucharist as the ultimate expression of God's love. And in response, we offer our total selves to God, willingly suffering any pain incurred in God's service.

Fourth Week

After living through the commitment, we seek the perfection of relationship. We want to be united with God unhindered by any weakness, fear, or self-centeredness. We meditate on Jesus' resurrection and his apparitions to his disciples. We walk with the risen Christ and set out to love and serve him in concrete ways in our lives in the world. We enter the contemplation of God's love.

Other Contents

Besides these essential Four Weeks, the Spiritual Exercises include guides to prayer, meditation, and contemplation. There are also useful guides for the retreatant. We will discuss some of the topics that we find most useful as the daily Examen, the Principle of Indifference, discernment, and guided prayer.

Repeated Use of the Spiritual Exercises

These growth cycles are repeated in one's life. With each repetition, we grow closer to God. Thus, St. Ignatius intended the Spiritual Exercises to be used repeatedly in one's life time just as an athlete would exercise regularly.

Resources for the Reader

We have included a glossary of Ignatian terms in the appendix. Readers unfamiliar with a term in the text can consult the glossary. The reader is asked to consult Fleming[2] and other resources listed in the Bibliography and the glossary of terms in the appendix for a further understanding of the Spiritual Exercises.

James Martin, SJ[3], says, "So if anyone asks you to define Ignatian Spirituality in a few words, you could say that it is:

1. Finding God in all things
2. Becoming a contemplative in action
3. Looking at the world in an incarnational way
4. Seeking freedom and detachment."

We have used the Spiritual Exercises to integrate those characteristics into our marriage.

Introduction to the Stages of Marriage

As a marriage educator formed in Ignatian spirituality, Bridget has observed for many years that the Four Weeks of the Spiritual Exercises of St. Ignatius and the Stages of Marriage parallel one another. Both the Spiritual Exercises and the Stages of Marriage describe the dynamics of human behavior in relationship.

The Four Weeks of the Spiritual Exercises describes a person's relationship with God — moving from seeking God, to allowing the relationship

---

[2] David L. Fleming, SJ, *Draw Me into Your Friendship: The Spiritual Exercises, a Literal Translation and A Contemporary Reading* (St. Louis, MO: The Institute of Jesuit Sources, 1996)

[3] James Martin, SJ, *The Jesuit Guide to (almost) Everything* (New York: HarperCollins, 2010) 10

to deepen and grow, and ultimately to being transformed by God's Love for us.

Likewise, in a marriage relationship we seek out a partner, enter a mutual commitment, live and grow in that commitment, and allow ourselves to be transformed. Both journeys start with seeking and follow similar paths to transformation.

Despite all our efforts to be knowledgeable as we enter marriage, many of us still enter relationship at a rather superficial level. In other words, we begin the relationship with much growth potential before us.

Marriage is a living dynamic. There is ebb and flow to the marriage encounter. Marriage educators describe this ebb and flow as the logical but not necessarily chronological stages of marriage. These stages are cyclical as follows. We begin in the "everything is wonderful" stage, then enter the commitment stage, followed by the disillusionment stage. We regroup and embrace living in the commitment stage and very gradually move into the transformation stage. Then we begin again. Each time we enter the marital cycle, we emerge more deeply committed and loved.

First Stage: the Pre-commitment Stage

At the beginning is the pre-commitment stage. In this logical first step, we recognize and awaken an innate desire to love and be loved. Whether, for the first time or after the end of another relationship, we risk vulnerability to date and to seek new relationships.

After an initial encounter, if the other person finds us attractive and wishes to relate with us, we experience bliss. Chemistry and infatuation blend to create the illusion of a perfect partner. We fantasize about our possible lovers (our Prince Charming or our Fairy Princess). We overlook their faults and we dream about life with them. This illusory bliss and fantasy is natural and normal. In fact, in the future, "the everything is wonderful memory" does much to move us forward through difficult times. Remembering what we first felt for our partner can pull us through when we are weighed down by inevitable disillusionments and disappointments.

Second Stage: The Commitment Stage

When we move beyond bliss and enchantment, we enter the second stage, commitment. As we learn more about our intended partner, our desire to love and be with our partner grows. We discover that we have fallen in love. This is the time to discern whether we are to marry. In the discernment process, we discover what fears are interfering with a free commitment to each other in marriage and gain the strength to sufficiently let go of our fears to make a free commitment.

Third Stage: Living the Commitment

We call the third stage "living the commitment." Various authors have described it as a time of "power struggle" and "disillusionment and disappointment." After perhaps an all-too-brief honeymoon, we awaken one morning to discover that we did not marry Prince Charming or Fairy Princess. In fact, we married someone who is pretty darn annoying! A significant number of marriages are lost in this period. But this stage can be a tremendous opportunity for growing and learning more about ourselves and our partners.

Faced with disappointments, the first person we try to change is our partner. Won't work! The only person we can change is ourself. Each of us needs to look at ourself and ask, "where am I and what am I struggling with?" The hard work of this self-examination can be facilitated by a third party, such as a relationship coach, counselor, or a spiritual director to guide us in sorting out the feelings of betrayal and disillusionment and to teach skills in communicating our dissatisfaction and frustrations, as well as our needs and wants. Some degree of dying to ourselves is required in learning how to deal with the conflicts and confusions that are part of any relationship. This aspect of that living out the mystery of marriage is living out the Paschal Mystery. Growing in intimacy calls us to a sharing in the dying and rising of Christ, from which we can emerge to more freely follow Christ in our married lives. (See the Third Week.)

Disappointments and conflicts occur, because most of us, if not all of us, enter marriage with some degree of brokenness, or woundedness, or lack of development in some areas of personality or just simply degrees of immaturity. We simply call it "baggage."

As the relationship unfolds, we bump up against the "baggage" in ourselves that we did not even know existed. We discover fears and insecurities that, prior to risking the intimacy of love, were dormant within us. As we move toward intimacy, obstacles to that intimacy begin to emerge. We look to protect ourselves, to circumvent the vulnerability that intimacy necessarily calls forth. Once again, we have the opportunity to grow and learn through this stretching. To honestly face our fears, our insecurities, and our anxieties and to share them with our partner takes tremendous courage and energy; but such honesty is essential if we wish to continue growing and if we want to be healed.

Our partner's love is a critical element in our being healed of "broken-ness." But first we must be willing to own our need for healing, and that is difficult. There is not much in our society that encourages us to turn within and to admit that we need to be healed.

Fourth Stage: Transformation

If we persevere in living the commitment, we will experience the transforma-tion stage. Through Christ, in Christ, and with Christ, our love is made whole and we move forward to become a sign of God's love in our world. In union with each other and with God, our joy and peace are beyond our hopes.

Circle of Love and Triune Union

Imagine marriage as a circle dance. Growth in life and relationship are cyclical processes. The Spiritual Exercises are a guide for what will work and what will trip us up as we endeavor to stay in the circle of love. They help us to discern the movements that lead us to union with the Trinity.

However, it must be stated that entering the circle dance of marriage requires stamina and commitment. Circles can swirl you, twirl you, and toss you off course.

Jerry and I have found that incorporating the directives of the Spiritual Exercises into our personal and marital lives supports us in being steadfast amidst the swirls and twirls.

The Triune God is the epitome of all relationships. All relationships have been created to move us toward union and communion with the Triune God. When, with God's grace, we have moved through the four stages of the Exercises, we will have come full circle. God's love initiates our journey, and at its end, draws us fully into the Triune Love. In our temporal world, we travel this circle over and over until ultimately, we are assumed into the Trinity, the Circle of Love Everlasting.

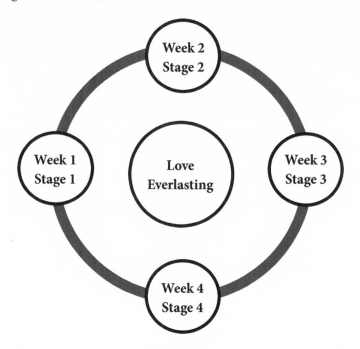

The relationship and intimacy of the Trinity is a mystery beyond human comprehension and experience. Yet in moments of marital intimacy, we seem to experience a glimpse of the divine intimacy. Thus, as in the Trinity, love begets love for the spouses and begets love for all those in their lives.

"The ability of human couples to beget life is the path along which the history of salvation progresses. Seen in this way, the couple's fruitful relationship becomes an image for the understanding and describing the mystery of God himself, for the Christian vision of Trinity, God is contemplated as Father, Son, Spirit of love. The Triune God is a communion of love, and the family is its living reflection." — Pope Francis[4]

About this Book

Being formed in Ignatian Spirituality, we write about what we know and have experienced. Reflection on our experiences using the Spiritual Exercises has greatly inspired and accelerated our spiritual growth as individuals and as a couple and has brought us closer to God and to each other.

On our marriage journey, we are influenced by the rapidly developing

---

[4] Pope Francis, *The Joy of Love: Amoris Laetitia.* (Washington, DG USCCB, 2016) 56

social and psychological understanding of relationship and especially of relationship in marriage. Bridget is trained as a marriage and relationship educator. We have given numerous pre-marriage classes and marriage enrichment workshops. This relationship knowledge helps us to understand our experiences, to realize that we are not alone in our struggles, and provides us with tools to strengthen our relationship. Putting these two influences together resulted in our book on the integration of Ignatian Spirituality and marriage.

Why We Write

Originality of Our Book

Much has been written and disclosed on both Ignatian Spirituality and marriage and relationship. But relatively little has appeared on the integration of marriage and Ignatian Spirituality. We feel that we can make a worthwhile contribution here.

Need for Our Book

> **At a time when more and more people consider spirituality and marriage to be irrelevant, we feel compelled to tell the world that there are still many who choose spirituality and marriage as the motivating forces for living their lives. And because of their choice, they are rewarded with lives of peace, joy, and gratitude.**

Therefore, we write on the integration of the spiritual and marriage life. As we grow closer to God, we also grow closer to each other. Our spiritual growth enhances our marital relationship. And our marital relationship enriches our spiritual life. This integration has led us to see that we are living holy and blessed lives and that we are helping to bring about the Kingdom. And this realization brings to us great joy, fulfillment, and gratitude.

We Hope the Book is Useful

We wish for others, especially married couples, to be aware of the holy and blessed lives they are living. We hope by telling our story that we encourage

others, especially you, dear reader, to tell your own stories. For that purpose, we have included reflection questions at the end of each chapter to
stimulate your own reflections. In our own life, sharing prayers and reflections have led us to encounters with God and with each other. And we
hope that you, the reader, also will receive the gifts of love, intimacy, and
joy from the Holy Spirit.

This book is our testament of our:

- falling in love with each other and with God,
- growing in love and intimacy,
- living out that love and commitment in our daily lives,
- going out of ourselves to serve others, and
- finding joy in being with each other and with God.

**Read this book as our story. Recall your own experiences as you read
our words. And let your own story take over.**

Our focus is on our relationship with ourselves, with our spouse, with
God, with the people in our daily lives, and with the world that we live in.
We begin by acknowledging that growing in intimacy is a gift, all of life
is gift, and all is grace. Although, the journeys to union with God and to
union with our spouse are concurrent and intertwined, and indeed, one
and the same journey, we have piece-meal experiences of different parts
of the journeys. It is only in reflection that we discover their concurrence
and integration.

Structure of the Book

Since the marriage journey to love and intimacy with each other parallels
the spiritual journey to love and serve God, this book is organized per
the logical process of the spiritual journey as expressed in the Spiritual
Exercises. Descriptions of the processes of marriage are matched to the
corresponding stages of the Spiritual Exercises. This match is illustrated
in the following table.

Stages in the Spiritual Exercises	Stages of Marriage
First Week: Preparing for God God calls us where we are. God's love allows us to let go of fears so that we can enter relationship with God.	**Pre-commitment: Preparing for Relationship** God awakens our desire to love. We gain basic wholeness and personal freedom that are required to enter marriage.
Second Week: Seeking Jesus We seek to know Jesus and his call to us. Out of love for Jesus, we commit to union with Jesus and his mission.	**Commitment: Seeking our Beloved** We respond to the call to marriage. We commit ourselves to live out the vision of marriage.
Third Week: Living as a Disciple We enter the passion and death of Jesus. We embrace both consolation and desolation. We gain the desire to make the necessary sacrifices to serve God faithfully.	**Living the Commitment: Living our Marriage** We experience the continual rhythm of dying and rising in our journey to intimacy. We make the necessary sacrifices to sustain the commitment and to grow in intimacy.
Fourth Week: Being with God's Love and Joy We desire being with God. We seek to be with the risen Jesus and contemplate God's love for us.	**Transformation: Being with my Beloved in Love and Joy** We are transformed day by day into greater union with each other and with God. We are energized to serve others.

In the body of the book, we bring together experiences and reflections from our marital and spiritual journeys to show their integration. We have selected parts from the Spiritual Exercises and offer our own reflections on them. We then discuss the impact of the spiritual growth gained from our reflections on our growth in our marriage. We also look at the various aspects of our marriage growth that have helped our spiritual growth.

As we share our own reflections on some selected exercises in the Spiritual Exercises, we invite the readers to do their own reflections on these selected parts. As we present our own stories and reflections of our marriage journey, we ask readers to recall stories and reflections of their marriage. Thereby the reader gains concrete and personal encounters with God and each other. We ask the reader to share these personal reflections with each other. We find sharing greatly enhances the emotional impact. While the book is not a substitute for a retreat, the reader can gain some personal experience of the Spiritual Exercises. And the reader can experience a marriage renewal inspired by the Spiritual Exercises.

Reflection

Throughout the book, we recommend the reader to reflect and to share.

Reflection is not something mysterious or hard to do. In fact, we do it all the time. To reflect on an event or encounter is to recall the event, to think about how it affects us, and to get in touch with how we felt at the time of the event and afterwards. Through reflection we seek to find the causes of what happened and the causes of our reactions, inactions, and feelings. Reflection becomes prayer when we ask God to help us distinguish between what leads us to God and relationship and what does not.

St. Ignatius distinguishes between two types of prayerful reflection. Meditation is a reflection that involves more thinking and contemplation is a reflection that involves more feeling. (See glossary.) Not making that distinction, all three terms — reflection, meditation, and contemplation — mean the prayful recalling, thinking, and feeling about an event or encounter.

Sharing

We risk vulnerability when we share something personal. Therefore, the listener should just listen attentively and not judge, criticize, interrupt, embellish, or respond. We should cherish the one sharing and what is being shared.

How to read this book

Our story is the transformation that we experience as we integrate our marriage with Ignatian Spirituality. Each of you has your own story of how you found God or how God found you. Concentrate on your own experiences, but let our experiences reinforce and enrich your experiences of God working in your lives.

There is no one way to read or use this book. Read it individually, read it as a couple, read it with other couples. Read parts of it, put it down, and pick it back up. There are no timelines. Nor do you need a guide to facilitate the book for you.

There are ample explanations in the text and additional resources provided in the glossary of Ignatian terms and a bibliography of books on Ignatian Spirituality, marriage, and other related topics.

Ideally, the best way to read this book is as a couple. To get full benefit from this book, use this book as relationship exercises for both your marriage and your spirituality. Use the reflection questions at the end of each chapter to merge the two; and through sharing, gift your spouse with your prayers, reflections, consolations, and desolations.

Set aside a little time, perhaps one evening per week, to read, pray, reflect on the questions at the end of the chapters. And then set aside time to share your reflections and prayers. Exchanging reflections gives insight into God's presence with us and God's action in each other. These are often moments of insight into our marriage where we experience love from a new perspective. The sharing involves us in mutual discernment and confirms or tempers our individual discernments.

Give Attention to Spirituality and Marriage Simultaneously

Married couples find it difficult to juggle the various parts — spiritual, marriage, family, work, and personal — of daily lives. In the busy-ness of our daily living, we seldom take time to work on our spiritual life or on our marriage. But both are crucial to our well-being. This book offers the opportunity to give attention to both.

Uniting the spiritual and marital also brings order and meaning to the other aspects of our living. Learning how to love each other teaches us how to love God and helps us to be grateful for God's love. What we do for each other also brings us closer to God. Through sharing, God's gift for one spouse is also given to the other. In living our spirituality, we inspire our children to live spiritual lives. Through integration, we can be "people for others" at the workplace and use our talents to build a better world. Even our time alone has meaning as rest and rebuilding for the journey to intimacy.

Inviting My Spouse to Read the Book

In circumstances where one spouse may be reluctant about reading and sharing, a gentle invitation can work wonders. All commitment to growth in relationship starts with an invitation whether from God or from another person.

Newly Married Couples Will Benefit from this Book

If you are recently married, you may not have personal experiences of some of the material that we have presented in this book. But this book is still for you. It will alert you to what you will experience later in marriage and give you greater understanding and appreciations of what may happen later, when it happens. The book may help you to face and resolve later issues. If you are married just a few years and have gone through a marriage preparation program, this book is an ideal follow-up marriage renewal.

Those New to the Spiritual Exercises Can Benefit from this Book

If you are new to the Spiritual Exercises and have not yet made a retreat, you can still read this book and grasp most of the meaning. We have tried to introduce and explain many of the topics and provide a glossary of Ignatian terms. But if the explanations are inadequate, don't let the technical terms or concepts slow or distract you. Just get to the heart of the meaning. This book is a good introduction to Ignatian spirituality — St. Ignatius' way of leading us to God. And if this book heightens your interest, we have provided a bibliography and an appendix of further resources.

Those Unaccustomed to Reflection or Sharing Can Use this Book

If you are unaccustomed to reflection, just start thinking and add in your feelings about an event or encounter. Bring God into the picture and you are doing reflective prayer. It is that simple and everyone does it even though they do not know what they are doing is reflection.

If you are afraid or unaccustomed to sharing, this book provides a safe and inviting environment for communicating heart to heart with your loved one. This book can be the start of lifelong sharing and conversation.

Others Also May Find This Book Useful

This book may be of interest to anyone who is seeking deeper spiritual freedom and more intimate relationships. We believe that the presence of God and the love we have found in our marriage can be operative for all intimate relationships.

This book also may be useful to small faith groups such as Christian Life Communities, Just Faith groups, and small parish groups. Spiritual directors and guides and pastoral ministers also may find this book useful.

Format

Chapter titles and major subheadings are aligned in the center. Minor subheadings are aligned to the left. Some contents are set apart from the body of the text for emphasis.

References

Each annotation — segment — of the Spiritual Exercises is given a number. Numbers in square brackets are references to the annotations in the Spiritual Exercises. We use David L. Fleming, SJ's, translation of the Spiritual Exercises.[5] References to Scriptural passages are given after the end of the passage. We use the New American Bible, Confraternity of Christian Doctrine, 1970. Other references are given in the footnotes.

---

[5] Ibid., David L. Fleming

II

Foundation for Commitment: We are Called to Love God and Love Each Other

Know that the Beloved of your heart is the Divine Presence.
Love created us, and we belong to the Most High.
We are born to be loving expressions of the Creator's plan. Ps 100[6]

Purpose of Our Lives and the Vision of our Marriage

After a set of preliminary instructions, St. Ignatius begins the First Week with the Principle and Foundation, in which he sets out the purpose of our lives.

Purpose of Our Lives

The way we live our spiritual lives is critically affected by our view of God, of the purpose of creation, and of the purpose of our lives as a part of that creation. In the Principle and Foundation, St. Ignatius states the purpose of our lives [23] as follows: "God loves us, creates us, and wants to share life with us forever. Our love response takes shape in our praise and honor and service of the God of our life."[7]

---

[6] Nan C. Merrill, *Psalms for Praying: An Invitation to Wholeness* (New York, NY: Continuum, 2002) 205.

[7] Op. cit., David Fleming

Vision of Marriage

Flowing from and consistent with the above view of God and creation, our vision of marriage is as follows: All human beings are created for loving and intimate relationships with God, our Creator. As married couples, we experience relationship with God primarily, though not exclusively, through our relationship with each other. We are called to be one with each other so that we can be one with God and allow all the creative possibilities that flow from our marriage commitment to unfold.

This vision of marriage is wonderfully expressed in the Vatican II document, *Guadium et Spes*. "Authentic married love is caught up into divine love and is directed and enriched by the redemptive power of Christ and the salvific action of the church, with the result that the spouses are effectively led to God and are helped and strengthened in their lofty role as fathers and mothers. Spouses, therefore, are fortified and, as it were, consecrated for the duties and dignity of their state by a special sacrament; fulfilling their conjugal and family role by this sacrament, spouses are penetrated with the spirit of Christ, and their whole life is suffused with faith, hope, and charity; thus, they increasingly further their own perfection and their mutual sanctification, and together they render glory to God." [8]

> **"Marriage is a precious sign, for when a man and woman celebrate the sacrament of marriage, God is, as it were 'mirrored' in them —. Marriage is an icon of God's love for us." — Pope Francis[9]**

Guide for Living Our Lives

The Principle and Foundation expresses the goal and purpose of our lives and serves as a guide to how we are to live our lives and to conduct our affairs so that we can find joy and fulfillment. It expresses the "central truth" of all reality, namely all that exists is created in relationship to God and that we and all creation find our true being when we embrace our proper relation to God.

---

[8] Austin Flannery, OP. (Gen. Ed.) *Vatican Council II: Constitutions, Decrees, Declarations* GS 48 (Northport, NY: Costello Publishing CO., 2007) p 220

[9] Op cit. Pope Francis

This "central truth" for our spiritual life is also the "central truth" for our marriage. They have the same objective — the union and communion with each other and with God.

Do We Accept the Principle and Foundation?

For many of us, the realization of this Principle and Foundation — that God loves us and we desire to love and serve God in return — is the natural response to an experience of being loved and the first step to conversion. But the process of conversion is long and continuous.

We come to believe after a lifetime of discernment. As children, we accepted the image of God and our purpose in life from the faith given to us by our parents and our Catholic education. This childhood image of God drew us to a faith in and desire for God. In later years as we grew in the experience of love and understanding of God, of self, and of relationship, our faith deepened and expanded. And now and in the future, our desire to love and serve God is still and will be expanding, and we will more deeply internalize and accept God's love.

Likewise, our vision of marriage was a response to love and grew over time. Falling in love, we began to see our marriage as a call from God to be one with each other. And over time, we came to understand that the perfection of marriage and all relationships is union with God, with all people, and with all creation. We see and desire this unity as the goal of our spiritual and marital journey.

Expanding Experience of God and of Relationship

For us human beings, the experience of God and relationship will always continue to expand. For we are finite beings and can never fully enter Infinite Love.

Dynamic Image of God

God is almighty, infinite, and unchanging. But as humans, we experience God individually and collective from finite perspectives. As our perspectives are constantly changing, our images of God are also changing, dynamic, and growing.

If the image of God is dynamic and growing, perhaps it may be better to not dwell on a static image of God from our past education. Rather, we can ask God to reveal God's image to us in ways that we can experience. We can pray to encounter a compassionate God if we are to be with a loved one who is undergoing cancer treatment. We can desire to be guided by a wise God when faced with tough decisions. We can ask for a God of peace when we must resolve a dispute among friends. We can ask for a faithful God when we feel weak and unsure of ourselves. Such prayers can lead us to St. Ignatius' dictum of "finding God in all things." When we express our desire and our need for God, we become more aware of God in the present and concrete circumstances. And at the end of the day, in our Examen[10], we can ask ourselves whether and how God was present. And from our daily experience of God, we will come to a dynamic and growing personal image of God. Asking God to be where we need God is the last step of the Examen as suggested by Jim Manning (p 34).

Awareness of God's Presence

(**Jerry**) Recently, Bridget and I had planned a Sunday of church and a jazz concert. As I had no worries on my mind and no list of chores to do, I prayed in the morning to a God of joy. After a roaring start, the musicians unexpectedly played the traditional Irish tune, "Danny Boy," as a tribute to a departed band member. At that moment, God answered my prayer and filled me with joy and brought tears to my eyes. Music often surprises me with joy, especially if it expresses sentiments that I am already contemplating. On that Sunday afternoon, I was treasuring the love of my Bridget and my sons. "Danny Boy" is a father's lament that the son must go off to war while he must abide. He does not expect to see the son again while he is still alive and hopes that the son will visit his grave. This most beautiful of Irish songs reminds me that love and joy are present even in separation and war.

Discerning Truth and Reality

Our purpose in life and our vision for marriage will depend upon what we accept as true and real about God, ourselves, and creation. What we discern to be our present reality will greatly influence our motivation, desires, and

---

[10] See p 33 and the glossary in the appendix.

our choices. From our understanding and conclusions about that Truth of creation and our place in creation, we make our life choices, form our image of God, and come to accept our life purpose.

If we see clearly and experience fully the beauty and the joy of the love of God and the love of each other, we will enthusiastically choose to enter and to grow in relationship.

But because of our wounded condition, we often do not see clearly and do not have the spiritual freedom[11] to enter love. Because of foggy vision and limited spiritual freedom, we can turn away from love and relationship and choose false values. The process of Ignatian discernment can help us to see more clearly and to grow in greater spiritual freedom.

Reality is Both Physical and Spiritual

Our personal reality is both physical and spiritual; but we experience the physical and spiritual in different ways. We use our head and our external senses to grasp the physical and use our heart and our trust in divine revelation to plumb the spiritual. We are distressed when our head and heart have conflicting conclusions, desires, and choices. We look for the peace and joy that come from the concurrence, integration, and harmony of the head and the heart.

Jerry's Conflict of Head and Heart

(**Jerry**) I remember my distress in our discernment to marry. My heart was passionately in love with Bridget. She was so beautiful, so gentle and caring, and she liked the same things that I liked: dining, travel, Irish and classical music, intelligent conversation. But my head had major reservations mainly about meeting my obligations as a spouse. The "until death do us part" was scary. Our friend, Tom Curry, SJ, guided us in our discernment. He was prophetic in reminding us that our marriage was not only for our benefit but that someday we may be called upon to promote marriage and relationship for the benefit of the community. This suggestion greatly eased my fear. My head and my heart could now place trust in the Lord, because if the marriage is doing God's work, then God will give me the necessary

---

[11] See the glossary for definition.

grace. This occasion is a clear recollection of receiving the grace of spiritual freedom in discernment.

"Seeing reality with the eyes of faith, we cannot fail to acknowledge what the Holy Spirit is sowing."[12] — Pope Francis

Silence

For many of us, especially for Jerry, the head dominates. We do rational analyses before we ask, "what are we feeling in our hearts." For those of us who think before we feel, our feelings are often lost. To get a better balance between feeling and thinking, we must at times suspend the thinking so that we can attend to what is in our hearts. This comes from the silence that we practice in our contemplations and prayers.

St. Ignatius says, "We, as retreatants, will profit far more from the understanding and love aroused by the grace of God within us than from the rhetoric or brilliant insights of a retreat director. For in a retreat, we do not find knowledge satisfying us, rather deep down tastes and feelings that sensitize us to what really matters."[13] [2]

"For where love is concerned, silence is always more eloquent than words." — Pope Francis[14]

Retreat Experience

(**Jerry**) As I have related in our first book[15], I asked God for reassurances for my future life after retirement. God's answer to my prayer was an experience of being loved by God and by Bridget.

Nine years later, I retired from my teaching job. I was faced again with fears of the future. I faced fears of growing old and losing one's abilities, fears of depression — these fears stemmed from my deepest fears of loss of relationship. My external senses wanted some reassurances from the Lord. This time, God's answer was Jesus' answer to the Apostles:

At the Last Supper, *Thomas said, "Lord we do not know where you are going, so how can we know the way? Jesus said, "I am the Way, the Truth, and*

---

[12] Op. cit., Pope Francis, *The Joy of the Gospel*, 35

[13] Op. cit., David L. Fleming, annotation 2

[14] Op. cit., Pope Francis, *The Joy of Love*, 6

[15] M. Bridget Brennan and Jerome L. Shen, *Claiming Our Deepest Desires: The Power of an Intimate Marriage* (Collegeville, MN: Liturgical Press, 2004) 39

the Life. No one can come to the Father except through me. If you know me, you know the Father too. From this moment, you know him and have seen him." Philip said, "Lord, let us see the Father and then we shall be satisfied. "Have I been with you all this time, Philip," said Jesus to him, "and you still do not know me? Anyone who has seen me has seen the Father, so how can you say "Show us the Father." John 14:5–9

As I read these words, a flood of experiences of being loved — by Bridget, my sons, my family, my friends — came over me. And in deep gratitude, I answered with all my being, "what more assurances do I need?"

In both retreats, God moved me with an experience of being loved. God's gift was that God's love and Bridget's love will be with me always.

Love, not "brilliant" insight, was my consolation.

Guided by Desire

Our journey to love and intimacy starts with the desire to love and be loved. This desire is placed in our hearts by the Creator so we can respond to the Trinity's desire to love us. This is the ultimate longing of our being. If we are to fulfill the purpose of our creation, we must ask God for the grace to awaken that desire to love and be loved.

Asking God for the desire of intimacy frees us to allow God to lead and direct our actions. We can trust that God will grant our desire to love and to enter relationship and intimacy. We can let God be in charge and show us how. We can let go of our fears and not judge results. What seems to be failure in our eyes may just be what God had intended.

(**Jerry**) I have personally witnessed the truth of the above statement in my life. What I deemed to be failure had led me to what God had intended. I desired to teach and do research at a university after completing my Ph.D. I applied at over 100 colleges and even junior colleges. But I received no offers. A friend obtained an interview for me at a St. Louis company. Within in a week, they offered me a job, which I accepted and kept for 28 years until early retirement. In my mind, the failure to get a teaching position was the Holy Spirit's way of directing me to St. Louis, where I met Bridget. I know my life would be quite different if I had found a teaching position.

In 2001, my company was bought out by another company. Thus, the company offered early retirement incentives to reduce the staff. After discernment with Bridget and my adult sons, I retired and found a position teaching chemistry to nursing students. I enjoyed teaching for 10 years. Some may call that luck; but for me, it was the Lord leading me and providing options for me. Our former CLC guide, Carl Hangartner, taught that "Jesus became human to provide us with options." God leads us to where we can be fruitful and find joy. This is an example of the Vine and Branches Gospel (John 15) in action. God, the vine grower, pruned me so I can bear more fruit.

> **In our personal experience, we can attest that the more we let go and trust God, the more we grow in intimacy.**

What is Intimacy?[16]

In today's world, the word intimacy means different things to different people. But the essence of the intimacy that we seek is rooted in the Gospel of John.

"Holy Father, keep those you have given me true to your name, so that they may be one like us." — John 17:11

Our call to intimacy, to oneness, and to unity with another is as profound as the union of the Trinity, one God yet three distinct persons. The Triune God, who is Love, is the essence of intimacy. In emotionally healthy relationships grounded in love, we evolve into becoming more than we have ever imagined. We are animated with the power and energy of Love.

Intimacy that unites us with each other and with God is very real. We tend to take it for granted when we have it, and certainly, we know when we do not have it. It is real and yet intangible. It is a mystery but not magical.

Intimacy grows over time, sometimes slowly and almost imperceptibly. But with God's grace, it does occur. Day by day, we are graced with the experience of mirroring Trinity in our lives.

God's grace builds on nature, which means that each of us must do our part to foster intimacy. We need to learn the ways, even small and simple ways, with which we can build intimacy between us, husband and wife. We know how to destroy intimacy, but we are less sure about how to build it. A

---

[16] Please also read Pope Francis' wonderful description of the qualities of love. Op cit. Pope Francis, *The Joy of Love*. P. 45–58.

stumbling block is that we take love and intimacy for granted, forgetting that it needs nurturing and nourishing.

Marriage therapist John Gottman[17] recommends that couples "turn toward each other" rather than "turn away from each other." It is the "take him/her for granted mode" that can cause intimacy to evaporate over time. We are so busy in the day that we collapse into bed by ourselves and miss the moments for turning toward each other. Being aware and desirous of each other allows us to turn toward each other even in our busyness. We can capture the occasions when both of us are in the proper mood to receive each other.

For the two of us, turning toward each other is especially difficult when we are angry or hurt. After an argument, both of us prefer to go to our corners and brood. In our early years, we were slow to move toward reconciliation. As we grew to trust each other more and more, the interval for our self-imposed separation has grown shorter.

Moments of Intimacy

(**Bridget**) Each couple finds or often stumbles upon moments of intimacy or rituals of intimacy. A moment of intimacy for Jerry and me came with the labor, delivery, and birth of our first son. After saying good night to a few friends who had joined us at our home one evening during the Christmas holidays, I noticed that I was having some unexpected pain. After phoning the doctor at 1 a.m., we had a very quiet drive — not much traffic at 1:30 a.m. — to the hospital. We spent the next several hours just being together — Jerry with his stopwatch in one hand counting the intervals between my contractions and with my hand in his other. The solitude of just Jerry and me surrounded by quiet led us to breathe in the sacredness and mystery of new life emerging. A new life is created by God and born of Jerry and me — sacred still moment!

At 7:36 a.m., we welcomed our son, Francis Xavier. It was just us and the medical team. No cameras, no videos. The same was true when we had our second son, John Paul. With someone watching No. 1 son, we headed to the hospital, this time at 5:15 a.m. — another moment of intimacy that belonged to just Jerry and me.

---

[17] John Gottman, *Seven Principles for Making Marriage Work*. (New York: Three Rivers Press, 2000) 80

As married couples, we all have "stories" and "moments" that belong only to us. When we travel as a couple, we find moments of intimacy because there are no other distractions — just us being together, enjoying the adventure, the new landscape. Sometimes it is as simple as walking to a nearby park after a first snowfall and savoring the beauty of the snow on the trees.

There can also be moments of intimacy shared with our children, other relatives, and close friends. There is nothing like a snow day to slow everyone down and hang out together.

Sexual Intimacy

Sexual intimacy is an essential element of married love and life, but it needs to be part of larger intimate relationship. Sexual intimacy spills over from the bedroom to intimacy in being with your spouse in various ways: spending a Saturday cleaning out a basement, walking through a park on a snowy day, taking a drive to enjoy the fall colors, sharing a tender moment while watching a movie, or even attending functions of our children together. These day-to-day moments in our lives contribute to intimacy. If we are building up intimate moments outside of the bedroom, sexual intimacy is enhanced and vice-versa.

> **Sexual intimacy reflects the attention and care spouses show each other in all aspects of their marriage.**

Qualities of Intimacy

In our first book[18], we discussed the following hallmarks of intimate relationships,

- mutual desire for intimacy,
- trust — sufficient trust to risk vulnerability,
- honesty — honest enough to share true feelings,
- fidelity — faithful to each other and to the marriage covenant,
- respect for each other in all areas of married life,
- openness, gratitude, generosity, forgiveness, and not harboring bitterness.

---

[18] Op cit: M. Bridget Brennan and Jerome L. Shen

Since that time, we have come to realize that a sense of humor has a special role in our marriage. Marriage is too intense a commitment not to have some humor to provide for some elasticity. What a couple find humorous may be personal to them. There are jokes, anecdotes, phrases whose reference and meaning only you and your spouse are privy to. If you would try to explain it to another, it would be lost on them.

We read the daily comics in our local newspaper and often share the ones that make us laugh. Over the years, we have mined various songs or words or scenes that bring laughter, for example, "there is a hole in the bucket, dear Henry, dear Henry"[19]. This is usually a lead-in for something that needs to be done in the house.

A shared sense of humor claims the relationship as your own, just the two of you. Being able to laugh together about your foibles and disappointments is a sign of the commitment and trust in the marriage.

Fruits of Intimacy

Commitment, desire, mutual effort, and the grace of God are required for couples to build these qualities in their relationship. But the effort is well worthwhile. For as we grow in intimacy, we will experience the following gifts:

- Courage to love
- Freedom to love unconditionally
- Wholeness in our life, knowing that we are where we belong and connected to God and to our spouse
- A worthwhile life lived with grace and appreciation for beauty
- Joy, the greatest gift of intimacy.

Qualities of Intimacy Enhance our Relationship with God

The qualities of intimacy needed in marriage also are desirable for our relationship to God. Fidelity, honesty, mutuality of desire, and humor improve how we pray to God. Fidelity in marriage is a manifestation of fidelity to God that extends to all aspects of one's life. Fidelity to God requires fidelity

---

[19] An old folk song in which Henry gives excuses to Lisa for not doing his chores.

in all our relationships, the highest ethics in the work place, and the highest morality in our personal actions.

Making excuses and hiding feelings are easier in prayer than in marriage because God does not immediately confront us as our spouse would. I (Jerry) know that, at times, I have not been totally honest with God. It is not that I was trying to hide something from God, who knows all; but rather that there were things that I was not ready to tell God.

Knowing our mutual desires in marriage helps us to align our desires with God's desires. After years of sorting out our desires, Bridget and I have settled on intimacy as our core desire. It is consoling for us that God also desires intimacy.

Humor, necessary for human relationships, is also helpful in our prayer. There are times both of us have asked the Lord, "Are you kidding? Do you really mean for us to do this?"

What is detrimental to marital intimacy also hinders our intimacy with God. Fear can reduce our trust in and openness to God. I (Jerry) was not totally honest with God because I did not fully trust God's forgiveness, and out of fear of abandonment, I continually need reassurances from God.

> **Human beings cannot be intimate with God without also being intimate with another. And intimacy between humans cannot be sustained unless we grow more intimate with God.**

"Anyone who says 'I love God' and hates his brother is a liar since whoever does not love the brother whom he can see cannot love God whom he has not seen." — 1 John 4:20

In Summary

Having reflected on our call to intimacy with God and with each other in marriage, we summarize with these two truths:

> **God is almighty, all good, and loves us. In response to God's love, we love each other and live on in God's love.**

Principle of Indifference [23]

Immediately following the Principle and Foundation, Ignatius gives us two valuable tools: The Principle of Indifference and the Examen. The Principle of Indifference gives us a basis for evaluating our available options. Ignatius's Principle of Indifference [23] in making choices follows logically from the Principle and Foundation.

Simply stated, the Principle of Indifference is: If our goal is intimacy with God and with each other, then all the other things on earth and all our actions and interior dispositions should be valued by whether they lead us to our goal or not. Any object, action, or disposition is desirable if it leads us toward intimacy. It is detrimental if it leads us away from intimacy.

This Principle is really a statement of spiritual freedom, in that we are free to choose those desires that lead us to intimacy and to let go of those desires that take us away from intimacy.

The traditional marriage vow is an excellent expression of this principle.

I, Bridget, take you Jerry to be my husband. I promise to be true to you in good times and in bad, in sickness and in health. I will love you and honor you all the days of my life.

I, Jerry, take you, Bridget, to be my wife. I promise to be true to you in good times and in bad, in sickness and in health. I will love you and honor you all the days of my life.

Our marriage vows are a statement that our love and intimacy are the primary values. And if necessary, we forsake all other values to love each other.

The Daily Examen [24-26]

The second tool is the Examen of consciousness. Ignatius urges us to make a daily Examen. This Examen of consciousness is different from the examination of conscience in preparation for confession. The Examen is taking time each day to suspend our physical senses and experience God in our lives with our spiritual senses. The recommended time for doing this is at the end of the day. We can then look at what occurred that day and see how God is touching us in the events of the day. We can then discern what is of God and what is not of God in our day. We can be aware of the places in our lives where we have not yet allowed God to enter. We can then pray for the desire and courage to let God be in our entire being. We can then be at peace entrusting all our problems and loved ones to God's care.

Ignatius maintained that the Examen is one of the most important spiritual exercises and should not be skipped. There is no one way to pray the Examen. But Jim Manney's[20] book on the Examen gives the following simple steps:

1. Ask God for light. I want to look at my day with God's eyes, not merely my own.

2. Give thanks. The day I have lived is a gift from God. Be grateful for it.

3. Review the day. I carefully look back on the day just completed, being guided by the Holy Spirit.

4. Face your shortcomings. I face up to what is wrong in my life and in me.

5. Look to the day to come. I ask where I need God in the day to come. It usually takes 15 to 20 minutes.

An alternative form of the Examen suggested by three religious women[21] is as follows:

A Daily Check-in

"Jesus, you have been present to me today. Be near me now.
Let us look together at my day. Let us look with your loving eyes ...
When did I listen to your voice today?
When did I resist listening to you today?
Jesus, everything is gift from you.
I give you thanks and praise for the gifts of this day ...
I ask your healing in ...
I ask forgiveness and mercy for ...
Jesus, continue to be present with me in my life each day."

---

[20] Jim Manney, *A Simple Life-Changing Prayer: Discovering the Power of St. Ignatius Loyola's Examen* (Chicago, Il: Loyola Press, 2011)

[21] Katherine Dyckman, SNJM, Mary Garvin, SNJM, and Elizabeth Liebert, SNJM. *The Spiritual Exercises Reclaimed: Uncovering Liberating Possibilities for Women.* (New York: Paulist Press, 1989) 148

Some helpful questions for the Examen are, "What was life-giving for me today? What was not life-giving?" Life-giving does not necessarily mean easy or successful. Also ask, "Where did I experience consolation[22] today? Where did I experience desolation?" These questions are another way of asking, "Where did I find God or not find God?"

Praying the Examen as a Couple

In married life, we often have a need for individual quiet time and reflection. But we also, at times, have a desire to share our reflections with each other. We have found that, at times, praying the Examen together as a couple sometimes works well and, at other times, praying the Examen individually works better. Listen to your heart.

We find it helpful to set aside a time to share our prayer. Knowing that we are to pray together is motivation to do our individual reflections beforehand. It is very valuable that our spouse knows what is in our heart. At times, we will both share consolation and at other times desolation. As a couple, if we continually share our consolations and desolations, we deepen the bond of love between us and discover God's presence in our shared lives. We grow in our commitment to be with one another in the good times (consolation) and the bad times (desolation).

A Shared Retreat

An advantage of doing a retreat as a couple is that we can share our reflections of the day. Before and after we were married, we went separately on individual retreats. On return, the one on retreat was eager to share many consolations while the one at home was more focused on the challenge of caring for children alone. That is why we cherished, to this day, the retreat we had together with our 1-year-old child. Our friend Tom Curry, SJ, was at that time the director of a retreat house in Kansas City. He had an open weekend at the retreat house and arranged for us to come. He even asked someone to care for our son during the day. But there was illness at the baby sitter's house, so our son stayed with us. We had the entire retreat house and the beautiful grounds to ourselves. We remember well the intimate

---

[22] Op. cit. David L. Fleming, Please see pages 248 to 255 for explanation of consolation and desolation.

moments with each other, with our child playing, with Tom during spiritual direction and at Eucharist. It was a retreat, a family vacation, an intimate visit with a friend, and a quiet time with God.

In later years, we also enjoyed retreats with our CLC community when we brought all our kids and a baby sitter. We went to places that would take families and where the children could play as in state parks. We packed our cribs, toys, strollers, diapers, and all the necessities of a family vacation. Amid all the cares for our children, the adults found time to pray and unite as a community. It was finding God as a community of families.

Chapter II Reflections

The following reflections may be helpful. They are intended for a person to do individually and then to share the reflections with each other.

Reflection 1

What are the desires that you have for your marriage now, this year, and for the rest of your lives together?

What desires did you have for your relationship at the start of your marriage? How have these desires changed?

Reflection 2

Jerry and Bridget strongly believe that the spiritual journey and the marriage journey intersect and over time blend into one.

Do you see some connection between your spiritual journey and your marriage journey?

Reflection 3

Do you agree with St. Ignatius' purpose of life? (Principle and Foundation)

How would you state your life purpose?

Reflection 4

Do you agree with our vision of marriage?

What is your vision of marriage?

Reflection 5 Qualities of Intimacy

What qualities of intimacy are most important to you?

Share those with your spouse.

Reflection 6

In sharing his story, Jerry says that his "head" dictates.
Bridget would say that her "heart" dictates.
What combination do you think you are?

Head/ heart   Heart/ heart   Head/ head

Reflection 7: Try doing the Examen. Share that with your spouse.

Reflection 8

What is your image of God?

Has it changed over time?

III
Entering Commitment: We Desire and Gain Freedom for Relationship

Prayer for Generosity[23] (Attributed to St. Ignatius of Loyola)

Eternal Word, only begotten Son of God,
Teach me true generosity. Teach me to serve you as you deserve,
To give without counting the cost,
To fight heedless of wounds,
To labor without rest,
To sacrifice myself without thought of any reward,
Save the knowledge that I have done your will.

The First Week of the Spiritual Exercises and the First Stage of Marriage

The logical first step — First Week of the Spiritual Exercises and the pre-commitment stage in marriage — toward committed intimate relationships is to get ourselves ready to enter relationships. This involves recognizing our desire to be loved and to love in return and having sufficient personal freedom and autonomy to commit to a desired relationship.

The First Week of the Spiritual Exercises leads us to recognize and accept God's love and free our hearts to love God in return. The corresponding first stage (pre-commitment stage) in the marriage journey is to recognize and accept our desire to love and to gain the necessary freedom and autonomy.

---

[23] Michael Harter SJ, *Hearts on Fire* (St. Louis, MO: The Institute of Jesuit Sources, 1993) 35.

The Grace of the First Week

St. Ignatius used the term "desired grace" to mean the objective because spiritual objectives can only be achieved through the grace of God. The desired grace of the First Week and the objective of the pre-commitment stage are the same: to prepare ourselves to enter relationship with God and with others. In our preparation, we strive to realize the causes of past failures and their detrimental effects on all our relationships, to be healed of our past wounds, and to be freed from fears that stunt growth in intimacy. We seek to gain a healthy concept of God and of ourselves and to awaken our desire to love. Therefore, we ask for the desire, the courage, and the generosity to make those changes in our lives.

To this end, St. Ignatius asks us to reflect on the occasions when we have failed (sinned) in our relationship with God and with others. He asks us to consider the consequences of our actions, omissions, and desires that hurt our relationships. In our recollection, we looked at missed opportunities for relationship because we were too afraid to risk vulnerability, at the deep hurts that we have suffered from rejections or from broken past relationships, at how we have hurt others, and at our regrets and "what ifs." We give attention to God's response.

God's Response to our Failings

God's response is always love and forgiveness. In Genesis, the divine response to human failure was not to end the relationship but to allow humans to have what they desired, knowledge of all things — including pain, suffering, betrayal, disease, natural disasters, and death. God awaits our return.

To enable the return, God sends Jesus, a person who will lead us to divine intimacy. We learn that our rejection will not break God's relationship with us; God endlessly seeks and waits for us to come back.

God's infinite and unconditional love cannot "help" but forgive and repair the broken relationship. That forgiveness is offered not because of our contrition but because of God's great desire to be with us, to forgive unconditionally 70 times 7 times and more.

We Must Allow Our Self to be Forgiven

But we must allow ourselves to receive forgiveness if we are to experience its effects. Both parties must desire and agree to repair a broken relationship. Our contrition opens the way for us to receive and accept God's forgiveness.

In the same way in the marriage journey, it is contrition and apology that allow us to ask for and receive our spouse's forgiveness. In the aftermath of conflicts, mutual forgiveness is the first step toward rebuilding the relationship. In the gospel of Luke (Luke 15:11–32), the parable of the prodigal son is Jesus's way of revealing God's forgiveness. In that parable, the father is the figure of God. The prodigal son insults and breaks his relationship with the father by asking for his inheritance and leaving. In his deep love for the son, the father grants his son's wish. For years, the father bears the pain of separation and longs for the chance to reestablish the relationship. But the father does not force or coerce, trusting that the son will wake up to their mutual love. Sometimes we hear God's message in unexpected ways. And in this case of the prodigal son, the unexpected was a famine that awakens him. And he finds contrition and returns to intimacy and rejoicing with the father.

Forgiving Each Other

The power to forgive each other and to receive forgiveness is a manifestation of intimate marriages. If we experience love and intimacy in our relationship, we will trust the relationship and gain the courage to forgive and to ask for forgiveness. If we realize that God has already forgiven us, we will be more willing to take the first step to restore the relationship. Spouses who are deeply in love will know the intense pain of separation and will more readily seek to come back to each other.

Receiving Forgiveness

We go through periods in our life when we are so down on ourselves, we beat up on ourselves. At such times, it may be easier to forgive someone else than it is to forgive ourselves. We often carry lingering guilt feelings with us, even when we are forgiven. Guilt feelings, residual hurts, self-reproach keep us from accepting forgiveness. These feelings lead to mistrusting the forgiveness that we have received. At those times, we need the gentle touch of our spouse and of our God to reawaken us to life and love. Contrition and apology allow our spouse to touch us in those times.

Forgiving ourselves is not a matter of making excuses or reducing our guilt. It is, rather, recognizing and accepting our guilt, seeing the effect of our sin and faults in our relationships and coming to genuine contrition. We do not actually forgive ourselves, but we risk vulnerability to seek forgiveness and make ourselves ready to receive it.

We must allow ourselves to be forgiven if we are to repent and reestablish our relationships. To the extent that we are still feeling mistrust, guilt, or self-doubt, we will be unable to enter intimacy. And if we do not heal the relationship with our spouse and our neighbor, God's forgiveness and healing cannot take effect in us.

Immersed in God's love, we see the true nature of our sins, which separate us from the one we love. When we realize how much we are loved by God and love in return, we truly feel the pain of anything that detracts or breaks the relationship with God; and sorrow for our sins will bring us to contrition.

Fears Are Often the Causes of our Failings

Often the causes of our failing are our fears. God created us in the divine image and likeness with a desire to love and be loved. But we also have deep-seated fears that we may not be lovable and that we may not be able to love in return. Those fears make us acutely sensitive to the pain of rejection and betrayal.

These fears, confirmed by our real or presumed experiences of rejection, prevent us from risking and entering intimate relationships. Too fearful to risk serious dating, some withdraw when another gets too intimate for comfort; others do not enter marriage at all, fearing commitment and loss of self. If we reflect on our saying yes to our marriage, we will see that all of us have had to overcome some fears to enter marriage.

Yet, for all of us, it is only in risking relationship and by asking the questions "are we lovable and can we love?" that we hear "yeses" to our questions. We will be loved, and we will love in return. When we receive forgiveness of our sins and faults and reconcile with our beloved, we discover true unconditional love. Being loved unconditionally draws us into intimacy and great joy.

Bridget's Fear of Commitment

(**Bridget**) When Jerry and I discerned that we were being called to marriage, I was terribly frightened. In fact, I cried for the four hours it took us to drive from Kansas City, where we had made the discernment, back to St. Louis. I was frightened because, when I was younger, I was in a "rescue" marriage where Bridget the super savior was going to rescue Joe, who struggled with addictions to alcohol and drugs. I had met him when he was in a dry, sober period, but soon he relapsed. However, as I was determined to rescue him and was convinced that all that was needed was love, I decided to marry him without seeking professional guidance. Needless to say, it did not work out. And, unfortunately, Joe succumbed to the effects of longtime use of alcohol and drugs and tobacco. It was tragic to see what happened to him. It was also a stark reminder that we cannot rescue another.

I had to work very hard to face the fear of being hurt again, of making another mistake. It was the grace of the discernment process that allowed me to go forward. If God were truly calling us to marriage, then the grace we needed to go forward would be provided. I had to relinquish my fear and trust God. It was a difficult struggle.

Some Types of Fears

We know that all God's children have "baggage" — wounds that need healing. What does some of that "baggage" look like? Most of it, when unpacked, will reveal fears — often unconscious — that drive us and determine how we live our lives. They may include fears of rejection, of abandonment, of being possessed by another, of failure, and of loss — especially of loved ones. Stemming from our deep fears of being unlovable and being unable to love, these fears can be very detrimental to relationships. The good news is that we are not bogged down with all the basic fears, but certainly we each have some.

Inordinate Attachments[24]

Bound up with these fears are what St. Ignatius calls inordinate attachments — habits, desires, and tendencies that turn us in on ourselves, making us

---

[24] See glossary.

self-centered and selfish. They are obstacles to the personal and spiritual freedom needed for intimacy. Some of these may be the following: needing always to be in control, irrational anger, false sense of superiority, substance abuse, and others. Since our call is to intimate relationships, we need to seek God's grace and our spouse's support so that we can let go of these inordinate attachments. In some instances, we may need to seek professional help.

Unconscious Motivation

Psychologists remind us that much of our behavior is driven by "unconscious motivation." That refers to hidden and unknown desires that are the real reason for our actions. In our busy, harried lives, we often are not aware of the hidden or unconscious motivations that are driving our behavior.

Although the psychological term was unknown to him, St. Ignatius of Loyola understood that humans often act out of unconscious motivation. Therefore, he resolutely required members of the Society of Jesus to do a daily Examen of consciousness to become aware of the hidden desires. The finding of where God is in our lives brings us to awareness.

Anthony de Mello, an Indian Jesuit who died in the 1980s, maintained that we are all "sleepwalking." We must wake up and get in touch with our deepest desires as well as our deepest fears. [25]

As couples, we enter the marriage covenant with unconscious desires and fears. Gradually over time, as we grow more intimate with one another and as we trust more deeply our mutual love, we become more aware of the hidden fears that we harbor deep within. We also grow more cognizant of our deepest desires. In a stable and committed relationship, we become secure enough to allow those deep fears and desires to unfold and surface.

Healing Power of Love

The wonder and power of the marriage commitment allows the love of our spouse to be an instrument of God's healing power. Being willing to accept and respect that our spouse has fears that do not make any sense to us is part of the healing process. Being able to put the fears on the table disarms much of their power.

---

[25] Anthony De Mello, SJ, *Awareness: A de Mello Spirituality Conference in His Own Words* (New York: Doubleday, 1990) 43

If we do not own our fears, they will control us. And if we are controlled by fear, we will not change for the better. One of the graces of the Spiritual Exercises is spiritual freedom —a state of being free from our fears so that we can grow in relationship.

> **Love casts out fear and empowers us to live a life of love rather than a life of regret.**

For You alone, my soul waits in silence;
    from the beloved comes my salvation.
Enfolding me with the strength and steadfast love,
    my faith shall remain firm.
Yet, how long will fear rule my life,
    holding me in its grip like a trembling child,
    in a dark and lonely grave?
Fears keep me from living fully, from sharing my gifts;
    it takes pleasure in imprisoning my soul.
Fear pretends to comfort, so long has it dwelled within me;
    truly, it is my enemy. — Psalm 62[26]

Temptations

Because of past wounds, we no longer see clearly the true goodness and desirability of God's love. Other desires — including temptations from the devil that prey upon our fears — seem more attractive to us.

Light and Darkness

In today's world, we are continually being bombarded with temptations to choose things that are not of God. Darkness wears an alluring dress, fading the light.

For many, monogamy is no longer a strong value. The temptation to be unfaithful surrounds us. It seems to no longer be a taboo.

Being honest and fair in our workaday world is often scorned by co-workers who get by with being dishonest. We are driven to make more money and to spend more money. Bigger houses and better cars are part

---

[26] Op. cit., Nan C. Merrill, 114

of the expectation. A general lack of respect pervades our society and has an impact on how we treat family members, neighbors, co-workers, and clients. When we are inundated by such false values, we turn to Jesus' standard for direction. Jesus says, *"I am the light of the world. Whoever follows me will not walk in darkness, but will have the light of life"* — John 8:12.

Avoiding Future Failings

Embraced by love, we find the courage to avoid the temptations of darkness and avoid future failures. A prayer at a recent Advent penance service was very moving. The sense of the prayer was this. "Lord, we are waiting for your coming to us. We know that there are things in our lives that cannot be in your loving presence. Give us the wisdom to know what they are and the courage to eliminate them from our lives." The power of love frees us to see more clearly, to distinguish true values from false values, and to remove the fears that hinder deeper intimacy. In the struggle to avoid sin, the positive motivation of enhancing our relationships is more effective than the negative motivation of hell.

Value of Positive Motivation

(**Jerry**) I learned the value of positive motivation from a major conflict with Bridget. We were on a vacation trip to Nashville eager to attend a performance at the Ryman Auditorium, the original home of the Grand Ole Opry. The occasion of the blowup was reserving a table at a restaurant. The cause was that I often get angry at people. I am overly sensitive to what I feel are disrespect, incompetence, and discrimination by those who offer services. On this occasion, I incorrectly heard the waiter saying that he would not serve us. I became very angry and acted badly, shouting and calling names. Bridget was very upset and embarrassed. We nearly parted that night. But God gave me the grace to see how my behavior had upset Bridget. I desired to repair our relationship more than I desired to protect my ego. So, I managed to put aside my ego long enough to apologize. And Bridget loved me enough to accept the apology.

Being prone to anger has been a long-term problem for me, perhaps stemming from low self-confidence in social occasions. The positive motivation of growing in relation with Bridget gave me the desire and courage to seek change. I met with a counselor and learned ways to avoid getting angry and to control the behavior when I become angry. The methods helped, and I am motivated to use these methods because I love Bridget. Facing this fear also helped my prayer. I no longer had to justify my angry behavior to God and can admit my guilt and accept God's forgiveness.

Healthy Image of God and of Self

Healthy Image of God

We must have a healthy image of God before we can enter relationship with God. If we have a perception of God as vengeful and judgmental, our experience of God may be more harmful than good. Before we can love God, we must accept to some degree that God loves us and desires our love. Otherwise, the relationship with God can become that of a "parent-child" or a "co-dependent" relationship. Instead of a relationship of mutual love, God becomes a parent or provider. We ask God for everything and become angry when what we want is not granted.

Autonomy and Healthy Image of Self

The social sciences tell us that a healthy self-image is required for healthy "adult-to-adult" relationships. The two bookends of marriage are autonomy and intimacy. We need a degree of autonomy before we can enter a healthy adult relationship with another. Otherwise the relationship can be "parent-child" or a "co-dependent" relationship.

Poor Self-Image from Our Family of Origin

Those who grew up in homes where one or both parents were controlling and/or manipulative, often will partner with someone who is also controlling and/or manipulative. Likewise, those who grew up in a home where one or both parents abused alcohol and/or other drugs will often unconsciously seek out a partner who is also addicted in some way. We tend to repeat family patterns. We seek the familiar.[27]

---

[27] For more information see Scarf, Maggie. *Intimate Partners in Love and Marriage.* (New York: Ballantine Books, 1987)

Rebellion against Family of Origin

A variation on this theme is the case of individuals who again deliberately choose a partner who is totally different from the family in which they grew up. It is a type of "rebellion." In the PBS series *Downton Abbey*, Lady Sybil married the chauffeur, and in the 1954 movie, *Sabrina*, Humphrey Bogart married his chauffer's daughter. Such rebellion often works out in movies, but not always in real life.

The more differentiated we are as individuals, i.e. the more autonomous we are, after we have separated from family of origin, the more likely are we to be open to partnering with a person who does not share the same baggage that comes from our family of origin. With such a partner, we can explore and discover new ways to navigate life's bumps and detours.

Fruits of Increasing Spiritual Freedom

Autonomy and a healthy self-image are the fruits of the grace of increasing spiritual freedom. As our spiritual freedom grows, we discover, claim, and walk more and more into our own truth. We more readily and more enthusiastically say yes to God's invitation and we unfold and evolve more and more into the unique being that God created each of us to be. Healthy relationships require some degree of spiritual freedom. And as our relationship grows, our autonomy also grows and matures.

In a healthy marriage, in which both adults have a basic healthy self-concept, a fruit of the marriage is that we are loved into being who we would not have been apart from each other. We are better together; our world expands, and we are energized to be "people for others."

Healthy Relationship with God

We have come to realize that what we have learned from our marriage relationship also applies to our relationship with God. A healthy self-image and letting go of fears also are needed for an adult-to-adult relationship with God. For example, a person with a poor self-image will seek a relationship that depends on God to do everything that she fears to do herself. A person with fear of abandonment will constantly need reassurances from God. These limitations to our marriage relationship also are detrimental to the experience of love and intimacy with God. And as we grow in maturity and intimacy with each other, we also grow in maturity and intimacy with God. The spiritual journey to union with God and the marital journey to union with each other are one and the same journey that requires the same letting go of fears, healing of wounds, forgiveness, and reconciliation.

Awakening the Desire to Love

Our God-given desire to love can lie dormant because we do not recognize love. Or the desire can be blunted by past rejections and wounds. An experience of love can awaken that desire. An experience of love can heal the past wounds. Love, then, energizes and frees us to seek another for commitment to marriage.

Chapter III Reflections

Reflection 1

Reflect on an occasion in your marriage, when you were lacking in your response to love whether by action or omission.

How did you come to realize you were lacking in that response?

How did you respond to that awareness?

How did your spouse respond?

How did God respond?

Reflection 2

Reflect privately on the great love you have received from your spouse and from God. In the light of that love, are there behaviors that you would like to change or eliminate and any behaviors you would like to enhance?

Reflection 3

Reflect on what fears may be dwelling within you. Try to share them with your spouse. Remember that when we share something deep within us and something that makes us feel very vulnerable, the listener is only to listen and not try to fix the fear or minimize it. But just to listen … .

Ask for the grace to see what fears and inordinate attachments (see glossary) may still be within you. Ask God to heal you of all that keeps you from growing more deeply in spiritual freedom.

- Fear of rejection
- Fear of abandonment
- Fear of being possessed by another
- Fear of failure
- Fear of loss — especially the loss of loved ones
- Inordinate attachments

Reflection 4

Take some couple-time to reflect on how, as a couple, you have "wrapped each other round with care and concern."[28] [5]

Think of occasions when you have each forgiven the other. Has your relationship grown stronger because of your spouse's forgiveness?

Suggested reading: John 15:9–17; Mark 15:66–72; Luke 15:11–31

---

[28] Op. cit., David L. Fleming, 9

IV
Commitment: We Make a Commitment to God and to the Vision of Marriage

Lord Jesus Christ,
help me to discover you as a living person,
who focuses and unifies all my desires,
and gives meaning to my life,
to the total gift of myself to you,
and the going out of myself
that this gift demands.[29]

The Second Week and the Second Stage of Marriage

After readying ourselves to enter love and intimacy, the second logical step is to seek the lover and to make a free commitment. In our spiritual journey, we seek God in the person of Jesus; and in marriage, we seek our lifelong mate.

In the Second Week, we move to contemplate Jesus and his call to us. We want to see, hear, feel, and know this Jesus who loves us and to respond with a commitment to love and serve God.

In the marital journey, we enter the commitment stage. We want to see, hear, feel, and know our lover, and to fall in love. We discern the call to marriage and we freely commit ourselves to marriage. We commit ourselves in marriage so that we grow in union with each other and with God.

---

[29] Op. cit., Marian Cowan, CSJ and John Futrell, SJ, 99

The Grace of the Second Week

In the Second Week, we ask for the grace to be so moved by Jesus and his call that we commit ourselves to Jesus and his mission. In the similar way, we ask for the grace of commitment to marriage.

Themes of the Second Week

There are two general themes in reflections of the Second Week. The first theme is on Jesus and his call to us as revealed in the Gospels. Following the first theme, the second theme is on commitment and the quality of commitment.

First Theme: Contemplation of Jesus in the Gospels

Christ the King and his Call [91]

This is the first meditation of the Second Week. St. Ignatius was a soldier serving his king before his conversion. Thus, it is natural for him to ask what kind of king will earn his loyalty and service. Formulating some idea of the kind of God that will win our hearts and minds prepares us to meet Jesus. And when we do meet Jesus, he will far exceed our expectations, hopes, dreams, and desires.

Before seeking a partner in marriage, many of us have some idea of what we want and hope for in a spouse. And having fallen in love, we will find that our lover far exceeds our expectations and hopes.

Reflections on Jesus

(**Bridget**) The following reflections on Jesus are very moving for Jerry and me, leading us to experience intimate moments with Jesus and with each other. These contemplations in the Second Week speak of intimate relationships with Jesus and among family and community. These passages all come from the Gospel of Luke. They are vivid and touching.

We encourage you to do your own reflections and make your personal encounter with Jesus.

The Incarnation [101]

With Mary's yes, the Incarnation was accomplished through the Holy Spirit, and God became human. Through Jesus, God touches us in our humanness and reveals divine love in a way that we can experience.

The Mysteries of the Annunciation and the Incarnation [101]: Luke 1:26–38

(**Bridget**) The Annunciation is my favorite mystery. Maybe it is a woman's thing. No one knows for sure how Mary came to hear God's word to become the mother of Jesus. One thing is apparent, Mary had an ongoing relationship with God; this was not a "speed dial and whoever answers is the one" type of relationship. Mary understood the Covenant God had with the Jewish people. In many ways, I think Mary knew enough to say yes, and yet also knew little enough to say yes. Have you not had the experience of saying yes to something and not fully realizing what you had just gotten yourself into?

Mary's yes was an unfolding yes. With God's grace, she continually walked through her yes. Did she have doubts and fears at some point? I think so. Most of us who have made commitments that are truly of God and that are beyond us have doubts and fears. Yet, placing her fears in God's care, she continued to walk into that yes.

"Being with"

Incarnation speaks to me of "being with." God was with Mary; Joseph was with Mary and Jesus. "Being with" is the sacrament of presence. Being with each other in the good times and in the bad, in sickness and in health, in affluence and in poverty, that is the meaning of Incarnation.

A few years ago, I visited a father and his daughter. She was in intensive care with a chronic illness. When I walked in and saw the father holding his daughter, tears came to my eyes; it was a "Pieta," father and daughter, the sacrament of presence.

For many of us, "being with another" is not that dramatic or traumatic: stopping in to see a friend in nursing care, checking in on an elderly neighbor, listening to a friend or relative as they grieve the loss of a job. Incarnation is God with us; and as God is with us, we are called to be with those whom God places in our lives. And in our marriage, a gift we bring to each other is being present — being with one another day in and day out. We celebrate the good times with one another and we hold each other in the times of sorrow and sadness.

The Mystery of the Visitation: Luke 1:39–57

(**Bridget**) Filled with the Spirit, Mary "goes with haste" to be with her cousin Elizabeth, whom the angel has told Mary is with child. We know the story well. Upon seeing Mary, Elizabeth tells us, "The child leapt in her womb." And Mary proclaimed her MAGNIFICAT: "For the Almighty has done great things for me, holy is God's name." Luke 1:49. A sacrament of friendship! Two women, filled with the Spirit, allow their hearts to break open to one another in joy.

Let's focus now on Elizabeth, another woman of faith, hope, and love. Like Mary and Elizabeth, I am convinced that we seek out and find like-minded people, people who share our values. Mary knew in her heart that she must be with Elizabeth. Elizabeth knew that she must be with Mary.

A Sacrament of Presence

- touching gently
- speaking lovingly
- being fully aware
- feeling heart to heart
- communion of God, my friend, and me

A Sacrament of Friendship

- accepting without reservations
- reaching out
- inviting in
- giving of self
- receiving of another
- joy of love
- pondering what God had done for each of the women.

In the Visitation passage, we see two women whose hearts overflow with love and joy. Each of these mothers will lose their sons in violent deaths. Still they say yes to new life, as do their husbands, Zechariah and Joseph. We can only embrace life. We cannot possess it.

Being with Corine at a Nursing Home

(**Bridget**) In my own life, I was gifted with being present with a close friend who was dying. After battling Parkinson's disease for several years, Corine's health declined to where she needed to enter hospice. I sat with Corine in those 12 days of silence. Corine had become unconscious by then. I experienced the sacrament of silence and the incarnational grace of just "being with" Corine as her body very gradually shut down and allowed her spirit to be free. I was humbled that just sitting there with Corine in silence spoke to me more than any words could. I reflected on the mysterious grace of friendship and how past decisions we made of where to live, what job to take, what group to join brought us to one another.

Like Mary and Elizabeth, we proceed with haste to be with one another in the unfolding of our lives with its many turns and detours. And in doing so, our hearts are filled with wonder. We also recall the role that both Joseph, who was betrothed to Mary, and Zechariah, Elizabeth's husband, played in this visitation account. They are not mentioned in this Gospel passage, but we as married women and men can imagine and understand that both Mary and Elizabeth had the support of Joseph and Zechariah. In this encounter, Mary and Elizabeth sang a Magnificat of joy, but Joseph and Zechariah were humming their own tune of joy and excitement.

Nativity [110] Luke 2:1–19

(**Bridget**) The second contemplation of the Second Week is that of the Nativity:

- Mary and Joseph seeking shelter so that Mary can give birth to Jesus
- the birth of Jesus
- the angels, the shepherds, and the Magi coming to give honor and praise.

Contemplation

Contemplation is simply as follows: Read the nativity scripture passage. You may be drawn into the mystery and find yourself interacting with the people as the mystery unfolds. Let it happen, but don't make it happen. Go there and be with the person who pulled you in.

- Mary nursing her son
- Joseph trying to make Mary more comfortable
- the angels speaking to the shepherds
- the shepherds deciding what to do
- the Magi offering gifts

Get into the scene, smell the hay, hear the animals, see the Christmas star. Stay there and be still. After the contemplation, ask yourself, "What were your feelings as you were there with the unfolding mystery?" What moved me? Where the Spirit leads is where God's grace is to be found.

Nativity Luke 2:1–19

(**Jerry**) The beautiful and moving Christmas story is always told in a peaceful setting. The great Christmas hymn "Silent Night" creates the enduring atmosphere of peace and intimacy. Yet, travel and childbirth are chaotic events even in normal circumstances.

Trials of Travel and Childbirth

I tried to be with Joseph and Mary on their journey and their preparation for their child's birth. If I were Joseph, I would be very worried. When stressed, I tend to think of the worst-case possibility, and I like to be prepared as much as possible. Joseph and Mary did not have time to prepare. They could not put off the trip until after the birth. I would be worried about transportation arrangements, hotel arrangements, doctor and hospital arrangements, etc. I would be worried about safety in travel and in the delivery. In the stable, I would be worried about food, warmth, and unwelcomed intruders — the animals and the shepherds.

Mary and Joseph Doing Their Best and Drawing Closer Together

Yet, Joseph and Mary did the best they could and were at peace. Where did Joseph and Mary find such strength and peace amidst all this turmoil? I believe they found the strength in their relationship. They trusted each other and God. Couples with strong, trusting relationships generally draw together when faced with adversity and couples without strong trust tend to pull apart when facing adversity.

Mary pondered it all in her heart. Mary allowed life to come to her, and she lived and enjoyed what was given her. I worry that life will pass me by if I don't seize it and live it in my way.

> **Peace and joy comes to me when I live the life that God has given me.**

We Can Safely Draw Near a Baby

Of all the ways that God can come to us, God chose to appear to us as a newborn baby. A baby is the most approachable and lovable human form. All of us want to hold and caress a baby. We can safely draw near and love a baby without fear of rejection.

The Good News of the Angels

The angels came to bring news of great joy to the shepherds. The news is not that the shepherds' lot in life will change, nor is the news about conquering evil and righting all wrongs, or even about the forgiveness of sins and eternal salvation. The news is that a baby has been born. The great news is of new life. The great joy is that our savior has come to be intimate with us and to dwell with us.

Jesus' Baptism, Temptation, and Calling of the Apostles [158–161]

In the meditation of these three events leading to Jesus' public ministry, we discover how Jesus intends to do his Father's will. These three events at the start of Jesus' public life are linked chronologically in the Gospels. Marian Cowan, CSJ, explained that this series of events represents Jesus coming to realize his true being. And from his being came his mission. Thus, through this meditation, we hope to see Jesus more clearly.

- Lord, grant that I may see thee more clearly,
- love thee more dearly,
- follow thee more nearly. [104]

In the Jordan, God assures Jesus of God's love and trust. God reassures Jesus of his divine and human being.

In the desert, Jesus realizes more deeply that his mission on earth is to reveal the Father's love. He is not a temporal king providing for his people and bringing about peace and justice. He is to gather the Father's people in love. And then, through love, peace, justice, and abundance will follow.

In choosing his companions, Jesus shows us how his mission will be accomplished. Jesus called those who were willing to enter relationship with him. Through their mutual love, the Love of God will be revealed. And through the quality of their relationship, we learn how to live in relationship.

Our Call to Discipleship

All three of the synoptic Gospels have a calling of disciples. Peter and Andrew are among the first called, followed by James and John and then later the others.

As married couples, we too have been called to discipleship. Our call and invitation to marriage is our call to mission. By living the marriage covenant, we reveal God to the world so that:

Our love for one another is a light to the world.

Our raising our children is hope to the world.

Our marriage and family celebrations are joy to the world.

Our caring for others is a prophetic voice to the world.

Discipleship is the fabric in our marriage in which we "respond to that love which first created us and now wraps us round with total care and concern."[30][5]

Jerry and I try to let this invitation set the tone of day for us. In everything that we do from the most mundane and habitual to the most

---

[30] Op. cit., David L. Fleming S. J., *Draw Me into Your Friendship*, 9

difficult, we remember that we are building the Kingdom of God. This gives us the motivation to live life enthusiastically and reminds us to let God be in charge.

Second Theme: Commitment and Quality of Commitment

The following reflections on the Three Types of Persons from the Spiritual Exercise ask the question: "what is the quality of our commitment?"

Three Types of Persons [149–156]

In this meditation, St. Ignatius asks us to consider three types of persons in their willingness to let go of their attachments to follow God more closely. St. Ignatius asks us to consider what kind of commitment we will make to God.

The First Type of Person

"The first type of person — 'a lot of talk, but no action.' This person has all kinds of good intentions but always remains so busy about all the 'things' that fill up life that death finds such a one still thinking about making a bigger place for God."[31] A yearning has been awakened in this person, but it is not yet strong enough to bring about action and commitment. Perhaps, such a person is weighing the cost of letting go. The attractiveness of the desire does not outweigh the costs. Such a person has not yet accepted the gift of generosity from God to allow him to let go.

The Second Type of Person

"The second type — 'to do everything but the one thing necessary.' This type of person will do just about anything but face the block that hinders an availability to God's gracious invitation. It is as if this person is negotiating with God, trying to buy God off. So, this type may do a number of good things during life, all the time avoiding the honest way of facing the real issue."[32] This type of person is one that has deep-seated fears that

---

[31] Ibid., David Fleming 117
[32] Ibid., Fleming 119

prevent him from letting go. He is not yet ready to face the fears. His faith and trust in God and in his spouse is still not sufficient to overcome his fears. So, he will do anything but face the fears, even asking God to allow him to not face the fears. All of us have had this type of experience when we are awakened to our fears, desire to let it go, but are deathly afraid to do so. Those of us, who allow God's grace to work in us, will find the courage to face those fears.

The Third Type of Person

"The third type — 'to do God's will is my desire.' This type of person makes efforts neither to want to retain possessions nor to want to give them away unless the service and praise of God our Lord is the God-given motivation for action. Thus, the graced desire to be better able to serve God becomes clearly the motivating factor for accepting or letting go"[33] When we trust enough to face our fears and when we become generous enough not to count the cost, we enter into being the third type of person. The third type of person is one who has gained the freedom to let go of his possessions. When we attain this freedom, we are free to use our possessions to fulfill our desire for intimacy.

Our Commitment Strengthens as We Gain Freedom from Fears

This meditation is on the stages of growth within us. As we gain freedom from our fears and deepen our love of God and each other, we become more and more the third type of person.

Jerry's Possessions

(**Jerry**) This reflection led me to reflect on my dearest possessions. My dearest "possessions" are Bridget, my sons, and my grandchildren. I realized that I cannot protect them or give them the joy that I desire for them. Giving these loved ones to the Lord resulted in the consolation that the Lord will give them all that I desire for them.

When I made the meditation, I did not realize that my propensity for irrational anger was also a possession that I had to give up. I realize now

---

[33] Ibid. Fleming 119

that God was asking me to give up that possession so that God can give me the gifts of Bridget and my family.

Commitment

The intended result of courtship (Second Week and commitment stage) is a commitment to union with God and to union with our spouse in marriage. Commitment is necessary for God's grace to work in us. Commitment allows us to risk vulnerability in giving ourselves to the beloved. The strength of our commitment keeps us faithful to the covenant and wards off temptations to abandon the relationship.

Quality of Commitment

In the reflections on three kinds of persons [149], St. Ignatius asks us to examine the quality of our commitment. Because we are on a journey to unconditional love, our commitment must also be unconditional and total.

Unconditional Commitment of St. Ignatius

In St. Ignatius' passion to love and serve God, he came to an unconditional commitment. He let God write the fine print. This is expressed in his offering everything to God in his Suscipe[34]:

> Take, Lord, and receive all my liberty,
> my memory, my understanding,
> and my entire will,
> all I have and call my own.
> You have given all to me.
> To you, Lord, I return it.
> Everything is yours; do with it what you will.
> Give me only your love and your grace.
> That is enough for me.

---

[34] Op. cit., Michael Harter 84

Minimum Commitment

Many of us may think that we are doing well as good Catholics by obeying the commandments, attending Mass on Sunday and holy days, and praying and confessing regularly. And likewise, we think that we are good spouses if we do only what we are expected to do — remaining faithful, raising children, sharing chores, satisfying sexual and communication needs of one's spouse. But the experience of unconditional love tells us that our commitment must be much more than the minimum standards. Our desires will not be satisfied with anything less than unconditional commitment.

And, once we have made the total commitment to God and each other, we must grow toward clearer vision and greater spiritual freedom. And in that growth, we must continually renew and deepen our initial commitment. That is the purpose of the Spiritual Exercises and of finding God in all things.

A partial or conditional initial commitment will impede our growth in intimacy. We cannot freely risk the vulnerability if we are holding something back. If we put escape clauses in our commitment, we will not gain the trust necessary for the relationship to grow. We will be looking for self-protection before risking vulnerability. If our commitment and our motivation are so weak and conditional, we will find that eventually we will not practice even the minimum standards of being a faithful Christian or a committed spouse.

Parable of the Sower

In the parable of the sower, Jesus tells us about the perils of limited commitment. This is the same message as that of the reflection of three types of persons.

"Hear the parable of the sower. When any one hears the word of the kingdom and does not understand it, the evil one comes and snatches away what is sown in his heart; this is what was sown along the path.

"As for what was sown on rocky ground, this is he who hears the word and immediately receives it with joy; yet he has no roots in himself, but endures for a while, and when tribulation or persecution arises on account of the word, immediately he falls away.

As for what was sown among thorns, this is he who hears the word, but the cares of the world and the delight in riches choke the word, and it proves unfruitful.

As for what was sown on good soil, this is he who hears the word and understands it; he indeed bears fruit, and yields, in one case a hundredfold, in another sixty, and in another thirty." — Matthew 13:18–23

> **Without an unconditional commitment, we cannot bear fruit on our journey of love and intimacy.**

Review of Commitments

Once a commitment is made, it is natural to question and review and renew that commitment over time.

(**Jerry**) During the early years of our marriage dealing with job, children, and struggles with Bridget, I asked myself, "Is this all there is to marriage?" The answer in prayer and discernment is yes, this and much more. Yes, we are to grow to know and love each other and to know God in our daily struggles. So, I reaffirmed my initial commitment.

Discernment: "Introduction to Making a Choice of a State or Way of Life."[35] [169–189]

Because, in the Second Week, we are invited to make a commitment to God, Ignatius includes the guidelines for making choices and commitments. These detailed guidelines are placed at the end of the Second Week to guide the retreatant in making a commitment. Both of us find discernment is essential in our lives. It is needed in big or small and in everyday choices. It is necessary to bring order and integration of our spiritual, marital, work, and social lives. Discernment for making choices is not the discernment of spirits that Ignatius describes later in annotations [313–327] (Discernment of the spirits are guidelines to help us recognize what comes from God and what does not.)

---

[35] Op. cit., David Fleming 133

Discernment

Discernment is a movement of the heart and mind that seeks to find how God is calling me now in my life. The two of us have used these guidelines many times, individually, as a couple, and even in groups. In our experience, a fruitful discernment results in free choices and commitments, the zeal to work with God to accomplish the commitments, and a trust in God that brings about peace and harmony.

Three Graced Moments for Making a Choice

A good moment to make a choice is when we experience an overwhelming sense that the choice is right and that we want to choose it. When a choice is so compelling and flows from a centered heart that is grounded in prayer and openness to the Spirit, we need not do any further rational or emotional analyses. Just go with it, as Mary did spontaneously in accepting to be the mother of God. Such an experience is also a confirmation that we are making the right choice.

Another good time for making a choice is when we are pulled between consolation and desolation toward a choice. Then we can discern what truly motivates us and what fears put us in desolation. Interior movements reveal more clearly God's call to us and expose the devil's temptations.

A third appropriate time for making a choice is when we are calm, neither in consolation nor desolation. At such a time, we can make rational choices weighing all the pros and cons and apply the Principle of Indifference.

When Not to Make a Decision

A time to postpone a decision is when we are in turmoil and desolation. Rather than making a rash decision under the influence of desolation, St. Ignatius urges us to postpone the decision. "Nothing good can be done in fear and agitation"[36]

---

[36] Op cit., Marian Cowan, CSJ. and John Futrell, SJ, 85.

Discernment Process

We can use the following process for making rational decisions when we are calm.

First, we start the process by stating, in general terms, the decision we want to make.

Second, search out all available options. Exclude only those options that take us away from God or harm our marriage. Do not rule out options that may be difficult or nearly impossible to implement.

Third, get in touch with our heart and mind. Sort the desires of our heart, realizing my deepest desire as an individual and of our deepest mutual desire as a couple. Sort our mutual values, listing them in order of importance.

Fourth, get in touch with our fears. Fears may limit our freedom to choose. Those fears may make some options seem too difficult or impossible.

Fifth, evaluate the options with our mind and our heart. List the "pros" and "cons" of each option. Express how we feel about each choice. Use our values and desires in determining the desirability of each option. In the evaluation, consult other people, especially those that may be affected by our decision.

Sixth, try the choice for a short time. Live and act as if you had made the choice and see how it feels.

Seventh, the final step is to make a commitment. From time to time, review the commitment and renew the commitment if it is still the right choice.

Attitudes for Discernment

We find the following attitudes very conducive to discernment:

To trust in God and in each other,
To be generous with our treasure, time, and talent,
To seek God's desire over our desire,
To be open, especially to surprises from God,
To trust that we do not have to do this alone, and
To be available.

Discerning as a Couple

In our experience, as spiritual guides, we find that many adults make significant decisions in their lives without the benefit of the grace of discernment. Discernment is not a passive "whatever God wants"; rather it is a meeting of the minds and hearts, God's and mine, to see more clearly and ponder more deeply where God is leading me or us, to discover a deeper experience of God in my life, and ultimately to know a more intimate relationship with God. Discernment is a grace given to an individual, a couple, or a community. Marriage offers us the opportunity to discern as a couple.

Marriage is the First Shared Discernment

The call to marriage is the first shared discernment for a couple. Marriage is clearly a "call from God," a vocation, and it needs to be discerned. If we enter marriage as a discerned "call," we set the stage to continue to use the discernment process in marriage and family. What often happens is that married couples do not realize how God has been leading them and working in their lives until some years into their marriage. Whether we discover God leading us into marriage or discover God in our lives after we have been married for a while is not the point. The important point is to become aware of God's presence in our marital and family relationships.

"Marriage is a vocation, in as much as it is a response to a specific call to experience conjugal love as an imperfect sign of the love between Christ and the Church. Consequently, the decision to marry and to have a family ought to be the fruit of a process of vocational discernment." — Pope Francis[37]

Factors Mitigating Authentic Discernment:

These are some factors that hinder authentic discernment for marriage:

- An undeveloped self — not a clear sense of identity of who I am and where I want to go
- Not sorting out our deepest desires
- Fear of losing myself

---

[37] Op. cit. Pope Francis, *Amoris Laetitia 37*

66

- Fear of loss of control
- Fear of displeasing others
- Fear of commitment
- Too busy to reflect or listen to the Spirit
- Fear of the unknown
- Driven by secular values

These are true for individuals as well as for couples.

Some additional factors that hinder discernment for couples or for a communal discernment are:

- Different visions for life
- Lack of shared values
- Divergent beliefs

Decisions Made by Couples

Some of the decisions married couples may face during their married years are: the number children to have, what schools for the children, which job, whether to relocate, when to move to a different home, how to care for an elderly parent or loved one, and allocation of financial resources. This is the "stuff" of our lives. The grace of discernment can guide us in these very significant and life-changing decisions.

Some of Our Discernments as a Couple

(**Bridget**) Below are some examples of when Jerry and I have used the discernment process.

Discernment to Help Doug

(**Bridget**) When our sons were in middle school, they were pretty settled, did their homework, played some informal sports, and hung out at home. They did not require the extraordinary care that children with various special needs may require. During Advent, we discerned as a family that we could, if invited, welcome a young man into our hearts and share our family time with him on weekends. A colleague of mine was the social worker at a residential center for special needs children. I approached her for some recommendations. She immediately had an idea. There was a young teenager living there who was 15, Chinese as was my husband, did not have any local family, and would enjoy being with us and our sons on weekends. We went through the discernment again with Doug in mind and decided to welcome him. So began our journey with Doug. Doug is now 41 and our journey with him has been up, down, and all around. He now has a stable job, lives independently in an apartment near us and is happy with life. Doug has taught us so much about life, about the challenges of special needs individuals, about vulnerability and simplicity and how we as individuals can make a difference in another person's life and he or she in ours.

Living Out the Discernment

(**Jerry**) Doug especially changed my attitude. At first, I tried to be his teacher, mentor, and parent. I tried to challenge him. I took him to counseling sessions. I would be upset when he could not or did not respond. One time I was very frustrated when Doug missed an appointment with me. I was angry that he should waste my time. Then it occurred to me that my time with Doug is important to God.

Renewed Discernment

(**Jerry**) Being a friend to Doug and helping him were hard for me. He was often unappreciative and thought he was entitled to what I did for him. A recent e-mail from him prompted me to discern again whether I am still called by God to be Doug's helper. I am not questioning the original decision but rather examining the decision in the light of new circumstances. I asked in prayer if I was the cause of the problem of Doug's behavior toward me. I asked if I was trying to hang on because my ego didn't want to let go. I looked for others who could take over and would be willing to take over. The answer in discernment to all the above questions was no. Therefore, caring for Doug was still God's will for me. This discernment gave me the freedom and the grace to carry on. I forgave and accepted Doug's apology and together we repaired the relationship.

Discernment Sustains Our Efforts

If we are to long sustain our efforts to reach out to others, we need to renew our discernment at regular intervals and especially, when circumstances change. The grace of discernment renews and enlivens our efforts for mission.

Discernment on Helping a Close Friend

(**Bridget**) About eight years ago, a very close friend of ours required nursing care due to advanced Parkinson's disease. Corine had never married, all but one of her siblings was deceased and her remaining sibling was much older and unable to provide her the care she needed. In a visit to Corine, we observed the decline in her health. We returned home knowing that something was stirring within us. At that time, we were in the middle of making the 19ᵗʰ Annotation of the Spiritual Exercises — a Spiritual Exercise in daily life, a yearlong prayer journey in which a person takes time from his daily life to pray each day and to meet with a spiritual director each week. In our prayer, it became apparent to both of us that we needed to consider inviting Corine to come to St. Louis for skilled nursing care and we would be her family. We met with our spiritual director, looked at all the implications as best we could ascertain. We confirmed that we were both willing to be a part of this call and that we were available. We wrote Corine and asked if she would be open to this. She replied immediately with a yes.

Three months later, we flew to Florida to bring Corine back to St. Louis where she lived out her remaining seven years at a skilled nursing center surrounded by her St. Louis friends and St. Louis family. Being with Corine called forth in Jerry and me strength and commitment and a fierce loyalty to our friend. It helped that Corine had a sense of humor. In those seven years, the three of us were graced with a triune friendship and relationship that could only be given by the Spirit. Corine's gentleness, calmness, and openness to God in her life washed over Jerry and me, and we learned at her bedside what a yes to God really means in daily life.

Discernment of Mission to Tanzania

(**Jerry**) A more recent discernment centered on our heading to Bukoba, Tanzania. Our discernment began with Bridget's visit to San Antonio. She stayed with Sr. Dot Ettling, who was the founder and director of Women's Global Connection, an organization that promotes the development of women in poor countries by helping them to start and maintain a small business.

At that time, Dot's organization was completing a project to improve the diet of children by adding soy flour to their diets. When Bridget mentioned that I have experience in soy protein, Sister Dot started a full court press to recruit me for making soy milk and to recruit Bridget for teaching personal development skills.

Factors in Our Discernment

Three factors were crucial in our discernment. First, Jesuit Father Carl Hangartner, our CLC guide, taught that Jesus came to give us opportunities. Bukoba was certainly a great opportunity to better the lives of many.

Second, Jesuit Father Tom Swift, our national CLC guide, said availability is an important consideration. We were certainly available at that time, as I had retired and Bridget could spare the time from her work.

Third, I was worried about the project to make soy milk. Here in the U.S., we need large expensive equipment, sanitation and quality control, packing, storage, shipping, labeling, and marketing. The Bukoba women had none of these. But another principle of discernment is not to consider how to implement the decision. Otherwise, we would not be inclined to choose difficult or seemingly impossible choices. Instead, we are guided to trust God with the means of implementation of any decision that we see as the will of God for us.

Results of Our Discernment

These considerations led us to risk the trip to Bukoba. I brought to Bukoba portable soy milk makers and equipment for canning the soy milk. The other necessary equipment was purchased in Bukoba and set up on a side porch of a small house. The women of Bukoba and I made it work. Now, they are the only makers of soy milk in Tanzania. A few years later, these women obtained funding, built a small plant, and obtained quality approval from the Tanzanian government. Thus, some of the poorest children in Bukoba, who normally would get only one meal a day, can get a second meal of soy milk and soy flour.

In the meantime, Bridget visited the women in the villages, teaching them skills for self-awareness and development. We are very grateful for this experience. With a little help from us and others, the women of Bukoba have built a business that will help the children and themselves as well. This is confirmation that our discernment was correct.

We share the above discernment experiences to help you understand that marriage calls us and provides us with numerous opportunities to serve others, to be for others in myriad ways. The marriage commitment expands our world. And through God's love and the love of our spouse, our lives become richer than they would have been without marriage.

A Discernment Guide is Recommended

As we stated earlier, the discernment process is not difficult, but a guide is recommended to make sure you are being honest with yourselves. Gather the facts — the pluses and minuses. Sit with that. As a couple, do you agree or disagree on the pluses and minuses? If the secular values of more money or more prestige are driving your decision, discernment will not work. St. Ignatius is the patron saint of "indifference." Indifference means it is neither good nor bad to take a job that will earn more money; it is not good or bad to move to a larger home; it is neither good nor bad to have three children instead of four. St. Ignatius would simply ask,

> **"What will lead you to the greater honor and glory of God?"** That is the question on which all discernment resides.

In general, a spiritual guide would say, "What is best for you as a couple, as a family is what will give greater honor and glory to God." That is not as easy as it sounds. We have many feelings around these various personal and impending decisions. As a couple, we do not always agree. This is where honesty and vulnerability enter the picture. I think most of us underestimate how difficult it is to be honest about what our deepest feelings are. And sometimes we are conflicted and really do not know how we feel.

Meeting with a spiritual guide trained in discernment is highly recommended. We learn to discern by discerning. If we are open, generous, and courageous, God will grace us with a discerning heart.

The Dance of Marriage

Intimacy can be elusive. We can think that we are doing everything correctly in our marriage and we can still be not satisfied. Something is still gnawing within us. Because we live in a world of countless movies and television shows in which people meet, fall in love, and, voila, live happily ever after, we too often have a shallow view of the workings of married love that brings forth intimacy.

Relationship experts remind us that we need to discern between the essentials and the non-essentials. We often fail to consider that each of us is a unique human being with our own unique personality, our own way of doing things, our own thinking filters, our own perspectives, and our own family upbringing.

When we are madly in love, we ignore these personal identifiers. We are too busy trying to impress our intended — being who we think she/ he want us to be.

As we settle into our marriage, our uniqueness begins to resurface. This is often when disagreements and misunderstandings evolve. This is normal.

However, as we go through this evolving process of claiming who we each are, we need to be gentle with each other. We do not change at the same time or in the same way. We are migrating toward being one yet distinct.

This is the basic dance step of marriage — becoming who we are as individual persons so that we can gracefully become more intimate with our spouse. Individual and mutual discernment is necessary for this growth.

Chapter IV Reflections

Reflection 1: Desires

How do my desires match with my spouse's desires?

Do I tend to reduce all desires to my desires and tune out God's desires for me and/or my spouse's desires?

Can I dispose myself to be "absorbed in God's desires" or is it still "all about me?"

What makes my response less total to God; what am I holding on to?

What makes my response less than total to my spouse?

Ask for the grace of discernment to truly know God's desires for me and not just my desires.

Ask for the grace of generosity to be open to my spouse's desires.

Reflection 2: Presence

Where in my life can I to be a sacrament of presence?

How am I present to my spouse, to my children, to my parents, siblings?

Sometimes it is easier to be present to my children than to my spouse.

Remember my spouse is my priority, the children follow.

Reflection 3: Joy

With whom can I share my moments of joy?

What have been some moments of excitement and joy in my life; in our life as a couple?

If you have children and when you found out you were pregnant with your first child, with whom did you share that joy?

Reflection 4: Mystery of the Annunciation, Visitation, and Nativity of Jesus

Ask for the grace to allow God to lead you individually and together to new places in your lives and in your hearts.

Annunciation Luke 1:26–38
Visitation Luke 1:39–56
Nativity Luke 2:1–20

Depending on how the Spirit leads you, go to one of the scenes listed above where you feel drawn. Sit there, be a part of the scene. What are your feelings; what attracts your attention; what do you notice?

If you have children, recall their birth or their coming to you through adoption. Can you identify with Joseph or Mary or Elizabeth or Zechariah or someone else in one of the Gospel passages?

Reflection 5: The Two Standards: Claiming Myself for Christ and Living Gospel Values

Ask for the grace to know Jesus more intimately, yourself more intimately, and your spouse more intimately; ask that you may know who you are and how to live out the Gospel values more clearly.

Throughout the Gospel, Jesus claims Who He is:
I am the Bread of Life. John 6:35
I am the Light of the World. John 8:12
I am the Good Shepherd. John 10:7–9
I am the Resurrection and the Life. John 11:25
I am the Way, the Truth and the Life. John 14:15
I am the True Vine. John 15:1
We too, must claim who we are.

Complete this statement: I am ...

For example, Bridget's is "I am a woman in love with life." And Jerry's is "I am one who has come to know the love of God." Being able to make an "I am" statement allows me to claim myself. Knowing who I am empowers me to discern God's call in my life.

Jesus was reflected in his values. His values helped to form him. What are your core values? Think of three to five core values that are the central to your life.

Please share your "I am" statement and your core values with each other.

Reflection 6: Discernment as a Couple

Think of a recent decision that you made together and the process that led you to the decision.

Are both of you satisfied with the process? With the decision?

What were the positive aspects of the process?

What are the negative aspects of the process?

What can you do to make the process better for the next decision?

Did you use a discernment process?

Did you experience the grace of discernment?

Did you experience God's presence in the discernment process?

Reflection 7

How has each of you evolved into your unique person?

How has being married to one another encouraged that?

Have there been some misunderstandings as each of you become more your "own person"?

For more information about personality differences see:
www.Keirsey.com
www.humanmentrics.com/cgi-win/jtypes2asp

Gary Chapman's *Five Love Languages* is also a good resource for learning about different relationship styles[38].

For more information about requirements, needs, and wants see our first book[39]:

---

[38] Gary Chapman, *The Five Love Languages: How to Express Heartfelt Commitment to Your Mate* (Chicago: Northfield Publishing, 2004)
[39] Op. cit., M. Bridget Brennan and Jerome Shen

V

Faithful to the Commitment: We Make Sacrifices to Grow in Love and Intimacy

From Death to Life[40] (St. Peter Faber, SJ)
Jesus Christ, may your death be my life,
and in your dying, may I learn how to live.
May your struggles be my rest, your human weakness my courage,
your embarrassment my honor, your passion my delight,
your sadness my joy.

Grace Desired for the Third Week

In the Third Week, we move from freely entering commitment to living out the commitment to Jesus and his mission. In marriage, we enter the stage of living out the commitment to our marriage vision. In both the spiritual journey and the marriage journey, we realize the hardships that must be endured if we are to honor our commitments. We realize that we need the power of God's love. We ask Jesus to allow us to join him at the Last Supper, in his agony, and in his death on the cross. We want to be with Jesus so that we "realize that Jesus loves me so much that he willingly suffers everything for my rejections and my sins so that we ask: 'What response should we make?' [41]

We ask God that our response be a desire to grow more intimate with Jesus and with our spouse. For that is Jesus' and God's desire and why Jesus made his great sacrifice.

In our marriage, we desire to experience mutual love so that we can

---

[40] Op. cit., Michael Harter SJ, 70
[41] Op cit., David L. Fleming, SJ, 151

bear the burdens together. We ask for the grace to live out commitments both in good, bad, and ordinary times. We ask for the graces necessary to let go of obstacles to intimacy, the courage to risk vulnerability, the ability to bear our pains and sufferings, and the compassion to bear the pains and sufferings of others. We ask for the awareness to see God's and our spouse's love for us and the faith to hold firm to our vision. We ask for these same graces from each other.

The Last Supper and the Passion and Death of Jesus

Living our commitments is challenging and difficult. We suffer the pains and sorrows and cherish the joys of life. By the grace of intimacy, we persevere through the pain and suffering and become more aware of our joys. St. Ignatius asks us to grow more intimate with Jesus at the Last Supper and in his Passion and Death. As married couples, we ask to grow more intimate in our struggles, pain, and suffering.

Judas and Peter

At the start of his Last Supper, Jesus showed his desire to love and serve by washing the feet of apostles. He then showed his love and forgiveness to Judas, who would betray him. By not stopping and condemning Judas at the Last Supper in front of the other apostles, Jesus forgives Judas for what he intended to do. Perhaps, even moments before the betrayal, Jesus hoped that Judas may still respond to his love.

Judas' response was not sorrow for his sin and a desire to repair the relationship. Perhaps, he did not have sufficient spiritual freedom to accept forgiveness. Instead of reconciliation, he chose suicide; and, thereby, he creates hell —- the eternal separation from love — for himself. We do not know why Judas killed himself. Perhaps, he could not live in the false reality that he had created for himself.

> **Hell is the creation of our free will and not punishment from God. God respects our decision to reject relationship with God.**

This theme is movingly presented in the musical *Les Miserables*,[42] based on a book by Victor Hugo. In that musical, Inspector Javert's justice-without-mercy world was shattered by Jean Valjean giving Javert his life. With all his convictions shattered, Javert ended his world by jumping into the Seine. He could not accept forgiveness.

Little Hurts Can Harden our Hearts

We say that we will never be like Judas. But we know that even little hurts, if not healed, can grow. and they will harden our hearts. And over time, we can become like Judas with a heart dead to love. Harboring even little hurts in our marriage over a long time can put a wall between the spouses and lead to the failure of the marriage.

Peter

Jesus also knew that Peter would deny him three times. Yet, in not admonishing Peter in front of the other apostles at the Last Supper, Jesus also forgave Peter. But, unlike Judas, with a heart fully in love with Jesus, Peter's response is great sorrow for his failure. He feels the pain of separation. And this pain drives him back to seek forgiveness and to repair the relationship. Peter's contrition allows Peter to receive Jesus' forgiveness and to allow Jesus to restore the relationship.

The Last Discourse

Partings and reunions are occasions when emotions of love swell in our hearts and we yearn to express our feelings. St. John's Gospel of Jesus' last discourse (John 13–17) contains some of Jesus' most intimate dialog with us. Jesus is about to leave the physical world and leave his disciples and return to God. His last words on earth show us the depths of his love. And God's love is revealed by Jesus.

---

[42] Alan Boublil and Claude-Michel Schonberg, *Les Miserable,* based on a book by Victor Hugo

Pray the Last Discourse

For the disciples, the Last Supper culminates three years of following Jesus, being with Jesus, and sitting at his feet to learn from him. They knew that Jesus was leaving them. They are worried, mournful, and agitated.

As you pray this gospel passage, imagine that you are a disciple at the Last Supper, seated with Jesus. Listen to the last discourse in the state of mind and heart of the disciples. Does your agitated state make it harder to experience Jesus' love? From the questions asked of Jesus, the disciples were more worried about Jesus leaving than about experiencing Jesus' love.

All of us know now that Jesus is still with us. We do not need to worry as the disciples did. Read John 13–17 again from Jesus' perspective, that of a father or mother or a teacher about to leave their loved ones. Feel and hear Jesus' last words to his beloved followers. Experience Jesus' love and care. Stay with any passage that moves you.

The following are our reflections on the Last Discourse.

Glory of God

"Father, the hour has come. Give glory to your son, that your son may give glory to you, inasmuch as you have given him authority over all mankind, that he may bestow eternal life on those you gave him. Eternal life is this: to know you, the only true God, and whom you have sent, Jesus Christ. I have given you glory on earth by finishing the work that you gave me to do. Do you now, Father, give me glory at your side, a glory that I had with you before the world began." John 17:1–5

What is God's Glory?

God's glory is union and communion within the Trinity, with us, and with all of creation. By his life and sacrifice, Jesus has made known God's glory to us. We experience God's glory and glorify Jesus by accepting the gift of union now and for eternity.

We see God's glory most intimately in our relationships. Our willingness to risk vulnerability, to seek and give forgiveness, to let go of self for the sake of intimacy and love, and our experience of joy are all manifestations of God's glory.

It is consoling that our growth in union with each other and with God adds to God's greater honor and glory.

Pain of Separation

As Jesus tells the disciples about his death, he realizes that their hearts are troubled and that they feel the pain of his leaving. The disciples as yet did not know of the Resurrection, so they must think his leaving is final. We know that Jesus has risen, but there is still the pain of separation. Jesus tries to reassure us, but he knows his reassurances do not lessen our pain.

"Do not let your hearts be troubled. You have faith in God; have faith in me. In my Father's house, there are many dwelling places. If there were not, would I have told you that I am going to prepare a place for you? And if I go and prepare a place for you, I will come back again and take you to myself, so that where I am, you also may be." John 14:1–3

Stories of Loss

Pain is intense when we lose loved ones. On those occasions, Jesus' words and being in solidarity with others who suffer loss brings some consolation.

(**Bridget**) Loss is a part of all our lives. We cannot escape it. We lose loved ones — parents, children, siblings, close friends, colleagues. Dying and rising are part of the cycle of life: the "paschal mystery." We have all faced it. We experience loss in many ways.

Some of us know loss at a very early age; others often not until they are into their adult years. We may know people who may have lost a spouse even before their child was born. How does a couple face a miscarriage? How do we get through the losses and eventually be healed of the loss so that we can go on living?

First, we need to recognize that we are grieving and that we need to be healed. Each person grieves in their own way on their own timeline. We cannot say to our spouse or to a friend, "It's been three months now, get over it." What we can do is be there with our spouse. Reverence and respect are what will aid our spouse to move toward healing. And our faithful and patient love will do much to allow our spouse to know God's healing love.

> **To paraphrase a well-known quote from Dr. Karl Menninger: Love heals. It heals those who receive it and those who give it.**

Jerry's Loss

(**Jerry**) Loss of a beloved is indeed very painful. Some years ago, I lost my dad to a heart attack. And ten years after my dad's death, I lost my mother and my sister in the space of one week. I try to let go of the loss and carry on the relationships in the absence of their physical presence. But I miss them and long to share my experiences and our sons and grandchildren with them.

Bearing Pain

Yet in my experience, bearing the pain willingly, letting go generously, and trusting God faithfully in times of loss is ultimately very consoling, worthwhile, and eventually joyful. For in those moments of pain and sadness, we experience more fully God's union and communion with us and our union and communion with our loved ones.

"I tell you most solemnly, you will be weeping and wailing while the world will rejoice; you will be sorrowful, but your sorrow will turn to joy." John 16:20

Bearing Pain Together

Although the promise of joy is comforting, it does not take away the pain at the moment of loss. Jesus is fully compassionate with us and experiences our loss. And out of his desire to be with us in all things, Jesus bears our pain in us, his body. Having someone bear our pain with us gives us the courage to hang on and bear the pain willingly. And hanging on will allow our pain to become fruitful through God's grace. We will then experience joy.

Compassion to bear pain together is a gift of a covenant relationship. As a married couple, we learn to be with our spouse as he or she experiences loss in his or her life. We cannot take away the pain of loss, but our presence is the gift that we share with our beloved. It is not solving a problem or trying to fix it but simply "being with." Accepting the vulnerability that we cannot take away the pain or suffering of our loved one, but, like Mary at the foot of the Cross, we can "be with" our loved one.

A Witness to Marital Love

(**Bridget**) A few years ago, Jerry and I came to know Joe and Vera. Vera was living at the same nursing center as Corine. When we met them, Vera had already been a resident at the nursing facility for a few years. Vera could not speak. She had to be spoon-fed. Did that stop Joe? No. He was there every evening, coming straight from work; and he would sit with Vera, wheel her into the dining room, and feed her. Joe was always upbeat and never complained about his wife. I do not even think the idea of complaining ever entered his mind. He loved Vera and was given the grace to "be with" her in her long suffering. He brought light and joy not only to Vera but to all of us who got to know him on his daily encounters. He was a witness to us of the grace of marital love.

We Do Not Know the Way and Show Us the Father

At the Last Supper, Thomas, in his anxiety, spoke for all the disciples when he said, *"Master, we do not know where you are going; how can we know the way?"* John 14:5

Like Thomas, we too want to follow Jesus to a physical place where we will be with him. But Jesus does not mean a physical place but spiritual union and communion with God. And we follow by growing in relationship with Jesus and with each other.

"To have seen me is to have seen the Father." John 14:9

Yes Lord, we do see your union with the Father through your words and actions but most especially through the love expressed in our marriage. Yes, we also see the union of married couples who show their love to each other and to their families. And we see that love and unity are passed on to the next generations.

When Will Our Day Come?

"On that day, you will not question me about anything. Amen, amen, I say to you, whatever you ask the Father in my name he will give you." John 16:23

And when will that day come? For the apostles, their day came after the resurrection when they finally understood and accepted that their union with Jesus will remain forever, even after physical death. And that day comes for all of us upon our acceptance of God's love and not later when we enter heaven.

For us, that day came when we said yes to the call to marriage. For our commitment to relationship put us on our journey to love and intimacy.

The Vine and the Branches

"I am the true vine and my Father is the vinedresser. Every branch in me that bears no fruit, he cuts away, and every branch that does bear fruit he prunes to make it bear even more." John 15:1–2

"I am the vine and you are the branches. Whoever remains in me, with me in him, bears fruit in plenty; for cut off from me you can do nothing." John 15:5

Again, Jesus reassures us. For we often wonder if our choices and actions are correct or if they will bear fruit. We are assured that any choice or action for love and intimacy will bear fruit and that God will lead and correct us so that we can be more fruitful.

Both of us are very grateful for God's pruning in our lives. We are grateful that we can see God leading us and that we have received the grace to respond. We have already seen some of the fruits brought about by God through our efforts. And we have grown to trust that as long as we remain in God and with each other, our labors will bear fruit even if they do not have the outcome that we desire. Now every day we remind ourselves that we are to do God's work and we do not judge the outcome by our standards. We cherish, especially, the work that we do together. We benefit from that work in growing closer together and knowing that we are called to do that work.

Remain in my Love

"As the Father loves me, so I also love you. Remain in my love. If you keep my commandments, you will remain in my love, just as I have kept my Father's commandments and remain in his love." John 15:9

The Gospel of the vine and the branches was our wedding gospel and "Remain in my love" was the theme of our wedding and of our lives together. It was the love of each other and of God that brought us together in matrimony. We have tried to honor all our commitments and made sacrifices to remain and grow in that love. We are grateful to God that he has led us through these 40-plus years, allowing the Holy Spirit to reveal God's love through our love for each other.

Your Joy Might Be Complete

"I have told you this so that my joy might be in you and your joy might be complete." John 15:11

The gift of joy is the greatest of God's gifts. It is the summation and culmination of all the other gifts from God. No words are adequate to describe joy. We cannot plan it, acquire it, or earn it. We certainly do not deserve it. It is purely a gift of God's love and union with us. We are often surprised by it. When we experience joy no matter how fleeting, we respond with deep gratitude.

We Pray for the Gift of Joy

As a couple, we pray and long for this joy from God. And we ask God to grant it as we grow in intimacy with each other and with God. We know that any effort and any sacrifice that we make in seeking intimacy will be worthwhile and that joy will make our lives worthwhile. We know with certainty that we will receive eternal joy because of Jesus' desire to give us this gift.

We pray also that all our loved ones will receive this gift of joy. We are concerned and pray for their well-being. But most of all, we pray that they receive and recognize God's gift of joy. For with joy, all other concerns are inconsequential. And because our joy will not be complete unless all our loved ones are joyful, Jesus' words assure us that all our loved ones will receive joy abundantly and our loved ones will join us in eternal joy.

We also pray that joy may be with you, dear reader, who, through reading this book, have joined us on the journey of intimacy.

Coming of the Advocate

"But I tell you the truth, it is better for you that I go. For if I do not go, the Advocate will not come to you. But if I go, I will send him to you." John 16:7

With the coming of the Holy Spirit, God becomes present to us both physically and spiritually. We are united physically with Jesus in the Eucharist and spiritually through the Holy Spirit.

John 17

(**Jerry**) For me, this is the most moving passage in all of Scripture.

> *"May they all be one.*
> *Father, may they be one in us,*
> *as you are in me and I am in you,*
> *so, that the world may believe it was you who sent me.*
> *I have given them the glory you gave to me,*
> *that they may be one as we are one.*
> *With me in them and you in me*
> *may they be so completely one*
> *that the world will realize that it was you who sent me*
> *and that I have loved them as much as you loved me."* John 17:21–23

Our most precious desire for union with God and our loved ones is one and the same as the glory of God, the purpose of our creation, and the purpose of Jesus' mission. What great consolation!

The Garden

In the garden, Jesus prays his last discernment. *"Father,"* he said, *"if you are willing, take this cup from me. Nevertheless, let your will be done, not mine."* Luke 22:42–43

Jesus so trusted the Father that he generously offers to do whatever the Father desires. Here in the last moment, he asks for confirmation and the grace to undergo his suffering and death.

It is not written in scripture, but God's answer here must have been the same as the answer given to Jesus at his baptism. The answer to Jesus and to all of us is always, "I love you. Trust my love."

Discernment Brings Peace

Jesus was agitated and in agony as he entered the garden, but he left the garden in a peaceful demeanor ready to face his trials. In our experience, peace and grace to embrace God's will are the fruits of discernment.

On many occasions, we have experienced the freedom and peace that comes with discernments that we have made together. Working through a process where we are open and trusting of each other allows us to find options that are mutually desirable. And having expressed our love for each other during the discernment, both of us can enthusiastically implement the decision.

God is Constant and Consistent

God chose not to take the cup from the Son. The Father is both constant and consistent. God gave human beings free will so that we can love and be loved. God will not compromise our free will even for the sake of the Son. For, if God coerced Caiaphas, the Pharisees, and Pilot to rule in favor of Jesus, all our freedom would be compromised. In not coercing those with power over Jesus, God allows the possibility that those who condemned Jesus may repent and receive forgiveness. God shows his love by allowing the natural consequences of our decisions.

Just as God does not coerce, married couples must not coerce each other. We can state our needs and request change. But we must not coerce.

Angry with God

In a lifelong marriage, we suffer many pains: loss of loved ones, broken relationships, illness, loss of financial security, and many more. When faced with these pains, we often ask God to remove them. But when God does not respond promptly, we ask why? We may even become angry with God. But if we can let go of that anger, we can hear God's response of "I love you."

Passion and Death

In willingly suffering injustice, torture, and execution, Jesus showed us that it is humanly possible to bear pain and suffering for the sake of love.

He shows that God's love is so powerful that it is possible to forgive his tormentors even while he is being tormented.

Through compassion, we ask Jesus to allow us to be with him in his suffering. And through being with Jesus, we hope to realize more deeply Jesus' love for us and express more sincerely our love for him.

In his passion and death, Jesus fulfills his promises made at the Last Supper in showing us the depth and power of God's love. Through his love, he gave us the desire and power to seek union with God and with all humanity. Through his sacrifice, he inspires us to accept God's love and eternal life.

Living the Paschal Mystery[43] in Marriage

The Third Week of the Exercises could be described as living out the choices in our daily life. And that describes the third stage of married life as well. In the first and second stages, you jump hook, line, and sinker into the Spiritual Exercises or into marriage. In the third stage, reality has arrived. The honeymoon is a blurred memory. The reasoning and realization of the Second Week and the second stage that led us to commitment falter as our "paschal mystery" emerges. In married life, the "paschal mystery" is central. Marriage, by its nature, challenges us to live the rhythm of dying and rising. It is the vulnerability of life and love that is so central to our lives. Whether in lovemaking, childbearing, or child rearing, we are not in control.

Freedom to Enter the Paschal Mystery

We are free. We must be free physically, emotionally, and spiritually to enter the "paschal mystery." Otherwise, we become enmeshed in unhealthy and unholy relationships. But, having embraced that freedom, we are tested and tried by circumstances of our lives: job loss, a difficult or chronically sick child, our own illness, needs of loved ones, relocation. The list is endless.

And yet it is in that crucible of the "paschal mystery" that we discover the deeper expression of the love of God and of our spouse. The foundation for living out the Third Week as well as the third stage of married life

---

[43] Paschal Mystery is Jesus, the Lamb, that is sacrificed for our sake and his resurrection to new life.

is love. Rooted, grounded, and embraced in the love of our spouse and of God, we emerge from the tomb freer and deeper. One passes from death to life. And spouses know that in whatever else may come, their fidelity to one another has been sealed.

The Healing Power of God's Love and the Love of our Spouse

In the "paschal mystery," we experience the healing power of love. As we walk along on our marriage journey, we encounter pain and loss. We cannot be alive and not face those challenges. We know that God's love is one of forgiveness and healing. Our spouse is also a source of healing. Love casts out fear and the love of our spouse can and does heal us of our fears. Our spouse's love also can heal us of earlier hurts and pain that we may have brought into our marriage. These fears may be hidden so deep within our being that we are not consciously aware of them. Marital love, rooted in God's love, is transformative.

Pope Francis[44] gives the meaning of the sacrament of Marriage in the context of the Third Week and of the third stage of marriage. "The sacrament (Marriage) is not a "thing" or a "power" for in it Christ himself "now encounters Christian spouses ... He dwells with them, gives them the strength to take up the crosses and so follow him, to rise again after they have fallen, to forgive one another, to bear one another's burdens."

An Example

We met a couple many years ago who shared a very personal and very moving experience in their lives. It spoke so much of the power of unitive love. They had lost their young adult daughter. We can imagine the terrible pain that this loss brought to them. When they returned to their home after the funeral, they clung to each other and entered lovemaking — the healing power of love.

---

[44] Op. Cit. Pope Francis, *Amoris Laetitia*, 37

Cycle of Renewal in our Loves

In his book, *The Holy Longing*, Ronald Rolheiser[45] speaks of a cycle of re-birth that mirrors the Paschal Mystery.

"1. Name your deaths — (Good Friday). What is it that you need to let go — loss of a parent, sibling, child, close friend, perhaps, the loss of a dream, a job, a marriage or relationship, or something else?

"2. Claim your births — (Easter Sunday) What is the new beginning that the Spirit is stirring within you?

"3. Grieve what you have lost and adjust to the new reality. (Forty days after Easter)

"4. Do not cling to the old. Let it ascend, and give it your blessing. (Ascension)

"5. Accept the spirit of the life that you are in fact living. (Pentecost)"

Rolheiser continues, "Christ spoke of many deaths, of daily deaths, and of many rising and various Pentecosts. The Paschal Mystery is the secret to life. Ultimately our happiness depends upon properly undergoing it."

Cycle of Rebirth

(**Bridget**) I can think of several "deaths" that I have faced in my life. A year after Jerry and I were married I gave birth to our son, Francis. Through discernment, Jerry and I had made the decision that I would stay home with our son.

It was wonderful and I am forever grateful that I had that option. Yet it was a letting go of my professional life, which I enjoyed and which gave me purpose and a sense of belonging. However, I gradually began to see glimpses of "new life" and "new opportunities" and to discover other parts of "me" that had not yet come to birth. And as I looked back over the years, I knew that the spirit of life had unfolded within me in a way it would not have if I had not let go of where I was.

A Second Experience

(**Bridget**) A similar experience happened to me just a few years ago. I had accepted a position with a religious community to serve as director of their

---

[45] Ronald Rollheiser, *The Holy Longing* (New York: Doubleday, 1999) 148.

volunteer program. I truly loved the position, the volunteers in the program, and the opportunity to grow professionally. It was a perfect match. But it was short-lived. Our son and his wife asked me to consider watching their 1-year-old. Well, that was a hard choice. I love children, always have, and certainly wanted to assist and support our son and his wife in their family life and their professional lives. After some prayer, reflection, and spiritual direction, I opted to leave the position and hang out with our 1-year-old grandson. The time with Gabriel has been exciting, expansive, and some days exhausting! But we have been present to each other in a way that is a gift for Gabriel and a gift for Grandma Bridget. Also, the person who took the position I had left was perfect for the job. Both she and I both experienced a letting go of "what was" to allow for "what would be." Each of us knows peace and joy in our discernment.

Living Our Holy Saturdays

Jesus died on Good Friday. His resurrection followed on Easter Sunday. In between, we are left to face Holy Saturday alone.

On Good Friday, we are shocked by the loss of our beloved. By Holy Saturday, the shock and pain have eased. We realize that he is really gone from our midst. Though Jesus promised that he would rise from the dead, our human senses cannot accept how that is possible. And we are faced with disillusionment, loss of hope, and fear of the future. We try to hang on to our hopes, to our memory of intimacy, and to our belief in Jesus' words; but the temptation is to give up in despair.

Hanging On

But if we give up as Judas did, our sorrow cannot be turned into joy and we will not know the resurrection. But we do hang on as did the disciples. We hang on because our desire for intimacy is so great and that desire will not let us give up in despair. We hang on because our hope is so strong that we trust Jesus' promises will be fulfilled even when we cannot see how. We hang on because the pain of separation is so great that we cling to any hope of renewing the relationship. We hang on because Jesus asks us to hang on. We hang on because we have made a solemn commitment.

And for the same reasons, we hang on to our marriage when we encounter Holy Saturdays in our marriage. And in hanging on, we sort through our experiences pondering them in our hearts, express our grief externally, reaffirm our commitment, and allow ourselves to be touched by love. Hanging on through Holy Saturday prepares us for the joy of Easter Sunday.

Holy Saturday Experience Allows God to Fill our Emptiness

This Holy Saturday experience is the prayer of the seventh day of the Third Week of the Exercises. St. Ignatius [298] asks us to let the effect of Jesus's death permeate our being. In a keynote speech at the 2011 Ignatian Spirituality Conference, Ron Mercier, SJ[46], said that "the seventh day holds us in a place where resurrection can happen and that we create a space for God by looking at our fears and desolation. Our emptiness of the day allows the risen Lord to enter in the Fourth Week."

Some Holy Saturday Experiences

Holy Saturday moments are a continuation of the Good Friday experience. There is a somber and sorrowful pall that hangs over. For couples, some of the Holy Saturday experiences may be trying to support and understand an offspring who has become addicted to drugs, alcohol, or other reckless behavior; to comfort family members who for whatever reasons have become estranged; or to face the long journey with a parent or other relative who has been diagnosed with dementia.

These realities last more than the "three days in the tomb." They may last three weeks, three months, three years or more. Yet, as Ron Mercier reminds us, this is the time that we can allow God to fill the emptiness of the Holy Saturday with the consolation of the presence of the Risen Lord. If we continue to place our trust in God, our Risen Savior will give us the special grace of experiencing and knowing God's consoling presence in our emptiness. Holy Saturdays are very difficult. But we should never underestimate the sustaining power of God's love, "wrapping us 'round with care and concern."

---

[46] Ron Mercier, SJ, *From Death to Life: Bridging the Third and Fourth Weeks* (St. Louis: Ignatian Spirituality Conference V, 2011)

Chapter V Reflections

Reflection 1

At the Last Supper, there is an experience of intimacy with Jesus and his disciples.

Have you experienced intimacy and joy when sharing a meal with your spouse, your family, and friends?

Reflection 2

What are some ways that you experience intimacy and joy as individuals, as a couple, as a family, or as a faith community?

Reflection 3: Compassion

How do you experience compassion with one another as a married couple?

Is it sometimes difficult to be compassionate toward your spouse or other loved ones?

Reflection 4: Presence

How do you and your spouse experience each other's presence?

Can you experience presence when you are not physically together?

Reflection 5: Passion and Death

How do you live out the "paschal mystery" in your marriage?

What experiences have you had in laying down your life for another, your spouse, child, parent, or other loved one?

Reflection 6: Holy Saturday

What have been some of the Holy Saturdays in your life?

Reflection 7: Healing Power of Love

What have been some of the healing moments you have experienced in your love and fidelity to one another?

How have your spouse's love and fidelity been a source of healing for you?

VI

Transformation through Commitment: We Enter Union with God and with Our Spouse

Being and Doing

When God calls us to union with God and with our spouse in marriage, we are called to a state of being rather than to action in service. But action flows naturally from our state of being. Thus, what is first is how we are with God and with each other in marriage rather than what we are doing for God and for each other. Doing cannot be sustained without strength that comes from the quality of being. It does not take married couples too long to realize that the quality of being together — feeling good about each other, trusting each other, enjoying each other — is much more important than what we do for each other.

Actions Flow from Being

But St. Ignatius reminds us that "Love ought to show itself in deeds over and above words."[47][231] Actions of love must flow from the gratitude for being loved and not from desire for personal gain. Depending on my motivation, the same action may have entirely different consequences. If our motivation is to return the love of our spouse, then we will come to greater intimacy and trust. If our motivation is selfish gain, then our actions will be manipulation of our spouse.

When we experience being with Jesus, we realize that all — life, love,

---

[47] Op. cit., Fleming

and joy — are gifts. And in gratitude we are motivated to give of what we have been given.

> **"For if we have received the love which restores our lives, how can we fail to share that with others."** [48] — **Pope Francis**

Grace of the Fourth Week

In the Fourth Week, we come to the culmination of the Spiritual Exercises and indeed the culmination of our journey of love. The grace of the Fourth Week is to be with the risen Jesus. Likewise, the culmination of our marriage journey is to be one with each other.

Contemplations of the Fourth Week

St. Ignatius asks us to contemplate the appearances of the risen Christ as described in the Scriptures. He also asks us to contemplate the risen Jesus visiting his mother after the resurrection. And finally, he ends the Spiritual Exercises with the Contemplation on the Love of God.

In the contemplation of Jesus visiting Mary, his mother, we desire the grace of being with Jesus in the joy and consolation of his resurrection. [221] St. Ignatius asks us to be there with Jesus and Mary and to enter their intimacy.

The Purpose of the Contemplations

The purpose of these contemplations is to lead us into an experience of intimacy, an experience of being. We cannot have intimacy on demand. But we can ask for the grace and prepare ourselves to be more receptive. God is continually giving love. Often, we are not aware or receptive of that love. Nor are we always aware and receptive of our spouse's love. So we try to prepare ourselves by being passive rather than active, being devoid of thoughts rather than thinking, being quiet and listening rather than speaking, being touched rather than touching so we can feel with our inner senses, closing

---

[48] Op. cite. Pope Francis, The Joy of the Gospel, 5

our eyes so that we can see with our inner sight, being unaware of anything so we can concentrate on being aware of each other and of God.

Seeing with Our Inner Light

Rembrandt, in his painting of the Return of the Prodigal Son[49], evokes a moment of great intimacy. As Henri Nouwen[50] explains it, Rembrandt painted the Return of the Prodigal Son near his death. It was the final statement of a tumultuous and tormented life. The blind father is a figure of the painter's aged self. Pain and suffering — he lost a son, two daughters, and his wife in a span of seven years — and the loss of sight has led the painter and the blind father to see with an inner light.

In the painting, the prodigal son does not look at the father. He, too, is seeing with his inner light. They are not speaking. But the son had rehearsed repeatedly how he was going to ask for forgiveness. The father, too, has many things to say to a son, whom he loves greatly. In such a moment, nothing needs to be spoken. Words cannot possibly express the emotions of the moment. All is said and experienced with the inner voice. They touch but they do not speak. They feel with their inner senses.

In this last Week, let us be with Jesus, Mary, and God. Let us be with our spouse in loving embrace. All is well and all will be well.

Please take some time to be with the risen Jesus and Mary.

Emmaus and the Sea of Tiberias

We conclude this chapter with two of our favorite passages from the post-resurrection Gospels. Both readings lead us to experience deeper intimacy in a way that was not possible before Jesus' resurrection.

Pray the following Gospel passages using your imagination. Imagination is a key concept for St. Ignatius. He is always encouraging us to imagine the scene that we are contemplating. See it, feel it, and be a part of it.

---

[49] The original is displayed in the Hermitage Museum in St. Petersburg, Russia.
[50] Henri J. M. Nouwen, *Return of The Prodigal Son* (New York, NY: Doubleday, 1992)

Emmaus (Luke 24:13–35)

Imagine that the two persons in this Gospel passage were a couple. We know the story. A couple was walking home the seven miles from Jerusalem, discouraged that the one, on whom they had placed their hopes, has now disappeared and they do not know what to believe. As the Gospel story continues, Jesus catches up with them and goes through all the prophets and more. The couple listens but still does not understand. They invite Jesus to join them for the evening to break bread with them. And in that moment of breaking bread with them around their table, the couple recognized him as Jesus.

Surprised by God

Talk about finding God in the surprise! They found God in the relationship of hospitality. Their hearts were burning within them while he had shared with them along the way. They look at each other, knowing that the risen Lord has been in their midst. They embrace, sharing their awe, wonder, and joy.

And what did the couple do? They rushed back to Jerusalem to the upper room to share with the other disciples what they had seen and heard. It is the Spirit dwelling within them that impels them to go forth.

We often find God in places we least expect as we journey along in fidelity and commitment.

> **If we can let go of our certitudes and agendas, we will find God in unexpected places as we walk together hand in hand.**

Our marriage covenant energizes us to move out to be a people for others, to share the good news of God present in our midst.

"Rejoice in the Lord always. I say it again, Rejoice" (Phil 4:4).

Sea of Tiberias — A Guided Contemplation John 21

Please let us guide you in a contemplation of the last appearance of Jesus to the disciples. This encounter occurred at Sea of Tiberias as told in the last chapter of John's Gospel. While remaining faithful to the meaning of the story, we have added some thoughts and feelings that increased the impact of this encounter for us.

We and the Apostles Enter this Contemplation with Different Perspectives

We enter this contemplation as post-Resurrection people. We realize that Jesus has conquered all our fears and failings and is giving his joy to us, now and for all eternity. We realize also Jesus is with us today, just as he was with the apostles on the shore of the Sea of Tiberias after the resurrection.

But the apostles have just witnessed the crucifixion, the empty tomb on Easter morning, and have seen Jesus in the upper room. The experience of resurrection has not yet set in. Their experience is still of loss: loss of hopes and dreams for God's kingdom and loss of relationship. They have walked with Jesus for three years. They have left friends and family to follow Jesus. They have come to love and be intimate with him. And they feel the emptiness.

So, they return home to something familiar, to fishing. Yet, home is no longer familiar, for they have been changed by intimacy. Nothing can replace that intimacy that they have had with the Lord and with each other. Jesus has sent them into the world to preach his gospel. Yet, they do not know what the future holds for them, what to do, and how to behave.

We are much like the apostles. Having worked, prayed, and shared through this book, we have been energized by the graces of the Spiritual Exercises and our reflections and sharing on our marriage, but we still face an uncertain future. What will we do? How will be we behave? Will it be the same? Or will we change for the better?

Please Come as an Apostle to Be with Jesus

Come now as an apostle and meet Jesus at the Sea of Tiberias. And after the reading, spend a few quiet moments reflecting on the experience. Use your imagination and see where you are.

Am I with someone or am I off to the side?

Is my spouse with me? Is there anyone else that I recognize?

What kind of day is it? Easter in Palestine may be cold.

The day is nearly over. Dusk is near.

How is the sea — calm or rough?

How am I feeling? What am I thinking? What am I doing? Am I talking?

Sea of Tiberias John 21

Later at the sea of Tiberias, Jesus showed himself to the disciples once again. This is how the appearance took place. Assembled were Simon Peter, Thomas (the 'Twin'), Nathanial (from Cana in Galilee), Zebedee's sons, James and John, two other disciples, and my spouse and me.

Having done nothing all day, Simon Peter said to them, "I am going out to fish." "We will join you," they replied, and went off to get in their boat. All through the night they caught nothing. Just after the daybreak, Jesus is standing on the shore, though none of us knew it was Jesus.

We did not recognize him because we were still blinded by our fear of loss and did not trust that he has risen and conquered death.

Jesus asked, "Children, have you caught anything to eat?"

"Not a thing," they answered.

"Cast your net off to the starboard side," he suggested, "and you will find something."

So, we made a cast, and took so many fish we could not haul the net in. Then the disciple Jesus loved cried out to Peter, "It is the Lord."

On hearing it was the Lord, Simon Peter threw on some clothes and jumped into the water. Meanwhile, the other disciples came in the boat towing the net full of fish. Actually, we were not far from land — no more than a hundred yards.

When we landed, we saw a charcoal fire there with a fish laid on it and some bread.

"Bring some of the fish you have just caught," Jesus told them. Simon Peter went aboard and hauled in the net loaded with sizable fish — one hundred fifty-three of them. In spite of the great number, the net was not torn. "Come and eat your meal," Jesus told us. None of the disciples presumed to inquire, "Who are you?" For we knew in our hearts, it was the Lord.

Recalling the Eucharist in the upper room, Jesus comes over, takes the bread and gives it to me and did the same with the fish.

As we sat eating the meal prepared by the Lord, none of us needed to ask "What is the way?" or "Show us the Father," or "What are we to do?" as we did at the Last Supper. For at this intimate moment, reality of the resurrection has finally touched our hearts and minds. And we finally realize that our relationship with God and with each other will last forever. No calamity, no earthly power, no loss, no betrayal, not death, not even our own sins can put asunder our relationship of love. And we sense that as long as we are together, we can face and conquer any challenge that the world has to offer. All that remains is to abide in love and joy.

When they had finished breakfast, Jesus said to each one of us "[My name], *do you love me?*" Answer Jesus from the depth of your heart.

[My name,] [My Spouse's name], "Do you love each other?" Both of us answer from the depth of our hearts.

At which Jesus said, "Feed my lambs."

A second time, Jesus asks, [My name], *"Do you love me?"* Answer Jesus from the depth of your heart.

[My name], [My spouse's name], "Do you love each other?" Both of us answer from the depth of our hearts.

Tend my sheep.

A third time, Jesus asks, [My name], *"Do you love me?"* Answer Jesus from the depth of your heart.

[My name], [My Spouse's name], "Do you love each other?" Both of us answer Jesus from the depth of our hearts.

Then we said, *"Yes Lord, you know everything. You know well that we love you."*

Then Jesus says, *"Because I can trust your love,* [my name] *feed my sheep."*

"I solemnly assure you, the man who has faith in me will perform the works I do, and greater far than these. Why? Because I go to the Father, and whatever you ask in my name I will do, so as to glorify the Father in the Son." John 14:12–13

"As the Father has loved me, so I have loved you. Remain in my love. If you keep my commandments you will remain in my love, just as I have kept my Father's commandments and remain in his love.

"I have told this so that my own joy may be in you and your joy be complete. This is my commandment: love one another as I have loved you." John 15:10–12

Chapter VI: Reflection

A moment of quiet with each other:

Please share some quiet time with your spouse.

To prepare yourself, get out of the way all the things that you have to do.

Put aside for the next few moments any problems that are on your mind.

Put away your watches so you are not tempted to keep time.

Then come together and hold hands.

Close your eyes and enjoy being present to each other and to the Lord. Don't speak.

Enjoy each other with your inner senses. Listen to each other with your inner ears. If you must think, think of how your spouse and God have been very good to you. Relax and take deep breaths, and sense God in your presence.

VII

We Live the Commitment in Our Daily Lives

In this last chapter, first we want to highlight some of the "nitty-gritty," everyday realities of married life. Second, we want to affirm that for married couples, evangelization and mission — reaching out to others — spring from our spirituality and our marriage. Third, we want to express our gratitude for the ways that the integration of Ignatian Spirituality into our marriage has transformed our lives. And finally, we conclude with sharing our hopes and dreams.

Everyday Realities of Married Life

Time

Each decade we are living our lives, "hurrier" and "hurrier." In today's world, where work trumps family, the norm is becoming such that we scarcely have time for "hello" and "goodbye." "Time is money" may seem terribly outdated to an Instagram, Twitter generation; but because time has somehow evaporated, we try to buy time with money. Too rushed to make coffee in the morning, we spend over $750 per year just having one latte a day. Too busy to pack lunch, we buy our lunch. There goes another $2,000 (conservative estimate): for a couple, that is $4,000. Too tired to go shopping, we shop online and just keep hitting the "add to cart" button. How rapidly our money disappears.

Work Trumps Time Together

In the initial honeymoon stage, we were attached at the hip. How does it happen that we move from being in the honeymoon stage to "becoming ships passing through the night"? It can happen. And it happens to most of us, if not to all of us, at some point. For many, work life has indeed eclipsed family life. Many adults are employed in jobs that demand more than an eight-hour day and 40-hour work week. Young couples often put in extra hours to prove themselves to their employers and supposedly build up job security. Since the recession of 2008, more and more employees are working longer hours and often more than one job to make up for job loss or to secure their financial holdings.

For some individuals, overwork becomes an escape to avoid the chaos or disharmony at home. We have a false idea that we can control our work life more easily than we can order our married and family life. We find our work more satisfying and less challenging than facing our problems at home. If we follow this pattern long term, we will miss the transforming power of marital love.

Sex

Love is not an express lane concept. Lovemaking requires nurturing and nourishing. Lovemaking is not an experience that can be checked off the list like shopping online. Women, especially need "be-fore play." Women need some personal space from working, picking up the children; fixing supper, etc. "be-fore" they have even the slightest inclination to want to make love. For couples beyond the workday cycle or without children in the home, women still need "be-fore" time.

But if we are stressed about time — how am I going to get everything done this weekend — and add to that the stress of being short on money and can't pay all our bills this month, romance tends to dissipate. We bring our arguments and stress into our bedroom. That is not good.

As adults living out a mission of dedication to the welfare of one another, of equitable and just distribution of our resources, of Gospel values related to time, of respect for one another, and of service to others, we are called to reclaim our time, our money/resources, and our lovemaking not only for our wellbeing as a couple but simply for the greater honor and glory of God. Living authentic lives *en toto* is how we give honor and glory to God.

Conjugal love points to and participates in a deeper kind of intimacy, a more than human connection to the ground of being. Through our spouse, we experience something that human creativity cannot manufacture.

Thomas Moore in his book, *The Soul of Sex*,[51] states: "The quality of our sexual experiences may depend on the ability to find the elusive but available middle place that is fully physical and fully spiritual, given over to passion and yet meaningful and expressive. Good sex requires that we leave ordinary reality behind by entering as deeply as possible into sensation, imagination, and passion."

Although Thomas Moore's book was written prior to the current "hook-up" era in which we find ourselves today, he distinguishes between marital sex and nonmarital sex in the following:

"[Marital sex] is richer, more complete, steadier, growing ever deeper unless it has fallen into an entropy caused by neglect. It [marital sex] gives rise to emotions and fantasies that are different from those occasioned by nonmarital sex. The latter may evoke more excitement, danger and the important and perhaps necessary feelings of anonymity. But marital sex has its particular pleasures as well: a fuller presencing of persons, the involvement of life, the security of faithfulness, a history of memories and fantasies, a greater contextualizing of sex that offers profound meaning and the opportunity for the development of sex as an art."[52] p. 217

It is up to us married couples to restore and refresh the powerful mystery and mystical experience of lovemaking and to reclaim lovemaking from the onslaughts of vulgar and disdained images of sex which pervade our media everywhere.

"The procreative meaning of sexuality, the language of the body, and the signs of love shown throughout married life, all become an "uninterrupted continuity of liturgical language" and "conjugal life becomes in a certain sense liturgical." Pope Francis[53]

Money

Many couples pair off as "spenders and savers." However, for successful married couples, responsible fiscal management is required. Savers need to be open to the spenders and discuss a reasonable and fluid budget. Spenders need to listen to the savers and try to understand their perspective. In fiscal

---

[51] Thomas Moore, *The Soul of Sex: Cultivating Life as an Act of Love* (New York: Harper Collins, 1998) 152

[52] Ibid., Thomas Moore 217

[53] Op. cit. Pope Francis, *The Joy of Love,* 105

matters as well as in other elements in married life, negotiation with respect and openness is the key.

The two of us make a budget each year. We review the budget and discuss various money allocations. We find that having a budget is not a constraint but allows us to move through the year with a sense of direction in spending. It is not about how much money a couple has; rather it is how the couple arrives mutually at how the money will be spent and saved. When two people work together and money is not used as a power or a control mechanism but rather as a joint resource, money issues dissipate.

Reassessing our Priorities

The issues of time, sex, and money are intertwined and cannot be faced separately. What do we do? We must sit down and reassess. Are the extra work hours really worth it? For what are we spending our money? Each couple must examine these issues closely and clearly. If an underlying value in our marriage is quality time with each other as well as with children, parents, or extended family, we need to make our time and money decisions that best align with our time together. Again, this is a personal discernment that each couple must make. In today's fluid world, we have many options. That's the good news. The not-so-good news is that we can push the options too far. The reality is that almost all of us are over-extended.

For the two of us personally, we check with each other before we make a commitment that is going to take us away from home for an evening, a weekend, or even longer. Before either of us made a job change, we sat down and reflected and discerned what the best outcome would be for us as a couple and as a family.

For many people, even on a good day or a weekend, finding and taking time for relaxed, uninterrupted lovemaking is a stretch. If you are empty nesters, what is your excuse? Just too tired or too caught up with your video games or shopping online?

Finding agreed-upon options to spend more time together, to enjoy uninterrupted lovemaking, and to attend to money matters can be challenging. Ultimately, we need the motivation, strength, and the generosity that spring from our commitment to the vision of marriage.

Conflict, Communication, and Commitment

The big three C's, as we refer to them — conflict, communication, and commitment — make up the superglue that holds our marriage together. Grace builds on nature. Think of conflict resolution, communication, and commitment as the conduits of God's grace ever guiding us toward a deeper union with one another and with God.

Conflict

If you meet a couple that says we never have any disagreements, be suspicious. It is the human condition to have conflicts.

Conflicts are normal. It is not the conflict that is the problem. It is how we resolve conflicts that either builds up or tears down the marriage.

There are differences of opinion, and there are conflicts. Differences of opinion are simply different views or perspectives. For example, when I drive to our parish church, I go one way. If Jerry is driving, he goes a different way. It is really immaterial which way we go because we get there in about the same time. Jerry and I both share household duties. Jerry washes dishes differently than I do. He folds the laundry differently than I do. We each complete the tasks responsibly, and life goes on. Because we are an extrovert/introvert couple, we differ at times on "how long is long," for example, when are talking with people after church. We negotiate.

Conflicts happen simply because it is natural for two people to have different ideas about topics that are very personal, e. g., money, family of origin, in-laws, parenting, the list goes on.

Anger Arises from Conflicts

It is difficult not to get upset and angry if my spouse is saying unkind things about my parent or sibling, or telling me I have spent too much money, or accusing me of not helping with the household chores. A key word here is "accusing." No one of us likes to be accused of something, even if we are guilty. There are ways to communicate to my spouse how I am feeling about having to go to his parents' house every Sunday without creating a battleground.

Facing Conflicts

Conflicts need to be faced. If we are really in a heated argument, we need to take a "time-out" and agree to come back to the discussion when we both have cooled down. We need to try to be open to what our spouse is saying, even if we do not agree. Try to see beyond the conflict. Try to see that you love each other and that you can both resolve this conflict. If the conflict continues to resurface over time, it may be wise to meet with an outside party whom you trust to assist you in resolving it. Sometimes, we just need a third party to facilitate the conversation. The presence of a third party in and of itself deflates the anger and helps each spouse calm down and listen.

Emotional Swirls

Ann Garrido in her book, *Redeeming Conflict*[54], has an excellent passage addressing strong emotions, our own and others'. Ann suggests that each of us has what she terms our own "feeling fingerprint," a unique set of emotional swirls that belongs to ourselves and to no other. Some of us have stronger "feeling fingerprints" than others. As individuals, we differ on how we feel about a particular idea or experience. Some people get irate if another driver cuts them off; another person barely notices. I used to get annoyed when the person in front of me in the express check-out lane (12 items or less) would have 22 items. I don't anymore. There are more serious issues to be angry about, such as homelessness, human trafficking, and war.

The essential note is that we are feeling beings. Some of us feel more deeply or more readily than others. Each of us as adults needs to be in tune with and in touch with our feelings. When speaking to our spouse, we need to express our own feelings. For example, I feel angry that … I feel sad that … I am anxious about … .

I not You

The key word is "I." I need to own my feelings, and I need to be able to articulate those feelings. Likewise, my spouse needs to do the same. Whether I agree with what my spouse is feeling or not isn't the point. The point is

---

[54] Ann M. Garrido, *Redeeming Conflict: 12 Habits for Christian Leaders* (Notre Dame, IN: Ave Maria Press, 2016)

I must listen and respect my spouse's feelings whether I understand the feelings or agree with the feelings.

An easy tip to try to understand more where our spouse's feelings are coming from is to ask her/him a simple, "Can you tell me more about why you are feeling that way?" We just listen; we do not say, "What you are feeling makes no sense to me."

(**Bridget**) Recently I shared with Jerry that I was getting anxious about a trip we had planned some months prior. I was becoming more and more anxious as the trip date approached. I realized two months after making the plans that it was too long a trip for me. Jerry listened intently. We explored options and were able to shorten the trip. The outcome was that I immediately felt relief. I am now very excited about the trip. And because Jerry accepted my feelings, he was not disappointed that we shortened the trip.

Communication

Communication is trickier than you think. Communication is not just talking. We all talk. And it is not just listening. It is listening with an open heart, listening with no agenda, and listening without an "I can fix it" outlook. It is listening and not judging; listening to not only the words but the whole person, his/her body language. And it is definitely not listening with our phone or video game in hand.

If we have learned to listen and be respectful of our spouse's feelings, we are well on our way to a healthy communication style. We humans, at least some of us, operate on the premise that what I have to say is so very, very important. We cannot wait for the other person to finish speaking so we can set everyone straight with our brilliance! That is called egotism.

Listening requires a lot of energy and self-sacrifice. It requires an emptying of self, so I can welcome the other person's words and feelings into my heart and mind.

Commitment

Commitment is the foundation from which our marriage grows. It is our mutual commitment to one another that allows us to risk vulnerability in the relationship, to risk being open to one another, and to sharing who we really are, not just who we think we should be. Commitment allows us to move forward, to be faithful during the struggles and the crosses that unfold in our own lives and in our married life. It is commitment that allows us to know it is worth the hard work and effort to keep our marriage intact and vibrant. Commitment is the shared umbrella under which we walk together in the rain and in the sun.

Living an Integrated Life

As married persons, we live a number of separate lives. We have a spiritual life that some of us relegate only to Sundays and brief periods of prayer. We have a married life that some of us often take for granted and spend little time and effort tending to it. We have a life with family, our children, and relatives, which for some is not a high priority. We have a social life with friends. We have our work life, which for some is the main focus. We also want to have some time for mission and evangelization. Finally, we try to find some time for a personal life that we can enjoy. Managing these seemingly different lives creates tension, anxiety, frustration, and dissatisfaction.

Managing Different Lives is Detrimental to Evangelization

Pope Francis sees this tension as detrimental to evangelization. "Today we are seeing in many pastoral workers, including consecrated men and women, an inordinate concern for their personal freedom and relaxation, which leads them to see their work as a mere appendage to their life, as if it were not part of their very identity. At the same time, the spiritual life comes to be identified with few religious exercises, which can offer a certain comfort but which do not encourage encounter with others, engagement with the world, or a passion for evangelization. As a result, one can observe in many agents of evangelization, even though they pray, a heightened individualism, a crisis of identity, and a cooling of fervor. These are three evils which fuel one another."[55]

---

[55] Op. cit., Pope Francis, *The Joy of the Gospel*, 40-41

Live an Integrated Life

How then do we juggle these separate lives? The simple answer comes from the spiritual purpose of life and the vision of marriage. The answer is to live one life.

Live a life of growing in union and intimacy with God and with each other. If we choose to live this life, everything else is a particular aspect of this life. We can then use discernment to determine the relative importance of each aspect of this life: spiritual, work, marriage, family, social, evangelization, and personal. We can assess how to blend each aspect so that our whole life moves us closer in union with God and with each other. And we can freely stop doing what is detrimental to our purpose. We can determine the relative time and effort that we need to spend on each aspect.

Focusing on intimacy with God and each other gives us motivation for action. We wake up and go about every activity with the knowledge and desire that we are doing it for God and each other.

The answer is straightforward and simple. But the application is not easy.

To live a life of love and intimacy requires growth in spirituality and relationship. It requires the constant and continual use of discernment, prayer and spiritual reflection, and marriage skills. With continual and repeated use, these skills will become habits. We start with a desire for an integrated life. But as we put that desire into practice, we will find that our life will be gradually transformed.

Mission Springs from a Healthy Marriage

Marriage is not a turning inward but a moving beyond our selves. Loved unconditionally by our spouse, we are energized to be a "people for others." Love begetting love, begetting love. The triune love of the Trinity dwells within us and between us and lifts us out of ourselves.

The marriage covenant is the foundation for mission. As a couple, we are better together. Not only are we energized by one another's love, but we are also there to support each other, to counsel each other, and to add a perspective.

Call to Mission is Unclear

As we endeavor to be a "people for others" (a strong theme in the Spiritual Exercises), we know the call to serve is not always clear; and sometimes the call has dangers and temptations. We need to check with our spouse before we make an outside commitment. Our first commitment is to one another, our children, parents, family, and from there we move outward. We cannot use mission as an excuse to avoid intimacy in our marriage or in our home. Each commitment to service needs to be discerned in light of our primary call to marriage and family. If we are faithful to our daily Examen and faithful to spiritual direction, we will receive the grace to build God's Kingdom beyond ourselves, on God's terms.

Exhortations to Evangelization from Pope Francis

In the *Joy of the Gospel*, Pope Francis has wonderfully proclaimed the meaning and context of mission in our Christian lives.

"Every authentic experience of truth and goodness seeks by its very nature to grow within us, and any person who has experienced a profound liberation becomes more sensitive to the needs of others. If we wish to lead a dignified and fulfilling life, we have to reach out to others and seek their good." [56]

"Life grows by being given away, and it weakens in isolation and comfort. Indeed, those who enjoy life most are those who leave security on the shore and become excited by the mission of communicating life to others."[57] — Pope Francis

"When the Church summons Christians to take up the task of evangelization, she is simply pointing to the source of authentic personal fulfillment. For here we discover a profound law of reality: that life is attained and matures in the measure that it is offered up in order to give life to others."[58] — Pope Francis

"Though it is true that this mission demands great generosity on our

[56] Ibid.., Pope Francis, The Joy of the Gospel 5
[57] Ibid., Pope Francis 5
[58] Ibid., Pope Francis 5

part, it would be wrong to see it as a heroic individual undertaking, for it is first the Lord's work surpassing anything we can see and understand."[59]
— Pope Francis

"The more you are motivated by love,
the more fearless and free
your actions will be." — Dalai Lama

Integration Has Changed our Lives

In our 40-plus years of relationship, we have gone through the weeks of the Spiritual Exercise and the stages of the marriage journeys many times. But as we live our daily lives, has there been any positive effect, and are we even aware of these growth cycles?

In our personal experience, the answers to the above questions are yes and yes. Through the grace of God and the many people who have encouraged, guided, inspired us by their lives, and loved us, we have changed for the better. Our relationships with God and with each other have grown. We realize that we are still far from that ideal to which we are called by God and by the Vision of Marriage. But we are joyful because we are making progress toward those ideals. In deep gratitude, we describe briefly the changes in our lives as a testament to many couples who live holy lives and to lead them to become more aware of the changes in their personal lives.

Our Vision Has Grown

First, our vision of the perfection of relationship (heaven) has been greatly expanded. We understand and feel more deeply in our hearts the joy of being one with the Trinity and with each other. That expanded vision is what we are now writing about. Our desire for the perfection of love and union has grown and is growing. And we sense that vision of unity is possible for us through God's grace and through our fidelity to our marriage. We experience that we are growing daily toward greater unity. We have faltered in the past and will falter again in the future. We know that we are a long way from Divine Intimacy. But, by our actions and desires and God's grace, we are on our way to heaven, the perfect union of God and God's creation.

---

[59] Ibid., Pope Francis 6-7

Trust and Faith in God and Each Other Have Grown

Our level of trust has grown, and we are more able to let go of our fears. I (Jerry) trust Bridget enough so that I no longer fear being abandoned by her. And Bridget trusts that I will not try to possess her. We trust God's love; and because of that trust, we entrust our loved ones to God.

Faith Has Grown

Our faith in God and each other has grown. As finite human beings, it is natural to ask, from time to time, "Is our belief in God correct?" and "Is our marriage correct?" As humans, we do not have absolute certainty. But we trust our experience, especially the gift of joy. We know that our experience is true. We experience a God of love and a marriage of love and intimacy. If not God and each other in marriage, we ask with Peter — *"Lord, to whom shall we go?"* John 6:68

Desires Have Become More Mutual

Our desires have become more mutual. It is not that we come to like the same things. Jerry is still an introvert, and Bridget is still an extrovert. But we understand each other's needs better. Jerry finds himself enjoying Bridget's many friends and Bridget takes more self-time. We have grown in our self-awareness and know more clearly what we truly desire. In our heart and head, we understand that our deepest desire — to be one — is mutual. But, we realize that we can be one without being together all the time and doing the same things.

Greater Awareness

We have a heightened awareness of each other and of God in our lives. We pray individually and together more regularly. We share and talk more often. We are more alive to each other. We are more aware and more accustomed to think of what our spouse needs and likes. And we laugh more together.

Positive Attitude

We have changed our attitude toward each other and improved how we negotiate our daily needs and wants. Through mutual trust, we are more able to listen without being defensive. We are more open to sharing our true feelings whether good or bad. We are more willing to listen to, to accept, and to appreciate our spouse's perspective on time, sex, and money. Rather than arguing and compromising our own wants and needs, we approach these issues as a team securing our present and building for our mutually desired future. We approach conflicts not to protect our egos but rather to seek reunion. We dwell less on our partner's actions that annoy us. And as a result, we find that we enjoy each other more.

Spiritual Growth

In our spiritual and marriage journey, we have grown from children accepting the Catholic faith from our parents, to teenagers and young adults eager to transform the world, to adults making sacrifices to raise and support a family, and finally to seniors still eager to serve while experiencing emotions of joy and gratitude.

We Trust Everything to God

We have come to trust that everything in our lives is given to reveal God's glory. More and more, we have grown to trust our most precious desires and possessions — our family and friends — to God. And more and more, we have come to experience God's love and glory. In bad times, good times, and in the mundane everyday times, we are less anxious and more trusting. And we are moved by joy and gratitude.

> We now try to live by these simple guidelines:
> Remember but do not regret the past.
> Accept the present.
> Let go of and change what is not of God.
> Keep and build on what is of God.
> Live without fear and trust all to God.

We share our spiritual journey, the journey of an insignificant couple made significant by God's grace given to us through the many people who have shared their lives with us. We share our gift with you in the hope that it will touch your journeys in some way. And if it does, then God's gifts are indeed given for the community, and they have achieved their desired effect.

Again, we thank you for reading our book, for keeping alive the Spirit of St. Ignatius, and for living a holy and transforming marriage.

With apology to Louis Armstrong, (*It's a Wonderful World*):

I see love of God, Bridget's, too

I feel love flowing for you and me

And I think to myself what a wonderful heaven

Our Hope for You, Dear Reader

Our hope for you is that you will know the transforming power of God's love as expressed through the love of your spouse, your family, and your friends.

We hope that you will come to realize that it is in the ordinary times of married and family life that God's love is revealed to us day by day.

We hope God will grant you a life filled with love and joy, now and forever.

Go forth and glorify God by the lives you are living.

Jerry and Bridget
AMDG

Chapter VII Reflections

Reflection 1: How do you balance time together, lovemaking, and money matters?

How are you addressing these issues if they are present?

How have you been able to integrate or blend your married and family life with your work life? Is it a challenge to keep home and work balanced?

Does Thomas Moore's reflection on lovemaking speak to you as a married couple?

Are you able to discuss your sex life openly and honestly with one another?

Reflection 2

Do you have recurring issues with conflict?

Are you able to resolve your conflicts amicably?

When you have resolved a conflict, do you experience a sense of freedom, peace, and intimacy?

Reflection 3

How are you communicating? Do you ask each other if you are hearing each other correctly? Do you paraphrase back to each other to make sure you heard what your spouse was saying?

Do you regularly sit down and share with one another rather than just wait until "we have to talk"?

Reflection 4

How has your commitment to one another grown over the years?

Was there "one moment" when the realization of commitment startled you to an awareness of yes, I/we are committed.

Do you see how a public commitment strengthens not just your marriage but the marriages around you?

Reflection 5

Do you agree that our marriage covenant grounds us, graces us, and moves us beyond our marriage and family to be a person for others?

How have you experienced mission in your marriage?

What has been your experience of discerning how God is calling you to be a "people for others"?

Mission is not an excuse for an unhappy marriage but the fruit of a happy marriage. Have you ever used mission as a way of avoiding marriage and family?

Reflection 6: Tips for Building up your Marriage (John Gottman)[60]

Nurture your fondness and admiration.

Turn toward each other instead of turning away.

Let your partner influence you.

Solve your solvable problems.

Overcome gridlock.

Create shared meaning.

Reflection 7: Daily Temperature Reading[61] **— A simple communication tool that we use weekly rather than daily:**

Share an appreciation with each other.

Share new information.

Puzzles — something you do not understand about your spouse.

Complaints or request for change (use "I" statement).

Share your hopes and dreams.

---

[60] John Gottman *Seven Principles for Making Marriage Work*. (New York: Three Rivers Press, 2000)

[61] PAIRS, *Daily Temperature Reading (PAIRS) Practical Application of Intimate Relationships Skills*. (Weston: Fl. PAIRS International)

VIII
Bibliography

Alphonso, Herbert, SJ. *The Search for Meaning through the Spiritual Exercises.* Mahwah, NJ: Paulist Press, 2001.

_____. *The Personal Vocation: Transformation in Depth through the Spiritual Exercises.* Rome: Editrice Pontifica Universita Gregoriana, 2002.

Arrupe, Pedro, SJ. *The Trinitarian Inspiration of the Ignatian Charism.* in Studies in The Spirituality of Jesuits 33/3, St Louis, MO: Seminar on Jesuit Spirituality, 2001.

Barry, William, SJ. *God's Passionate Desire and Our Response.* Notre Dame, Ind.: Ave Maria Press, 1993.

_____. *Finding God in All Things.* Notre Dame, Ind.: Ave Maria Press, 1991.

_____. *Paying Attention to God.* Notre Dame, Ind.: Ave Maria Press 1973.

_____. *Letting God Come Close.* Chicago: Loyola Press 2001.

Berends, Polly Berrien. *Whole Child/ Whole Parent.* New York: Harper & Row, Publishers, 1983.

Bradley, H. Cornell. *The 19th Annotation in 24 Weeks for the 21st Century.* Philadelphia: St Joseph Press, 2002.

Brennan, M. Bridget and Jerome L. Shen. *Claiming Our Deepest Desires: The Power of an Intimate Marriage.* Collegeville, MN: Liturgical Press, 2004.

Browning, Don S. *Marriage and Modernization: How Globalization Threatens Marriage and What to Do About It.* Grand Rapids: William B. Eerdmans Publishing Co., 2003.

Burke-Sullivan, Eileen and Kevin F. Burke. *The Ignatian Tradition.* Collegeville, MN: Liturgical Press, 2009.

Cahil, Lisa Sowle. *Women and Sexuality: Madeleva Lecture in Spirituality.* New York: Paulist Press, 1992.

Chapman, Gary. *The Five Love Languages.* Chicago: Northfield Publishing, 1992.

Cowan, Marian CSJ and John C. Futrell SJ. *Companions in Grace: Directing the Spiritual Exercises of St. Ignatius of Loyola.* St. Louis: The Institute of Jesuit Sources, 2000.

Curtis, Brent and John Eldredge. *The Sacred Romance: Drawing Closer to the Heart of God.* Nashville: Thomas Nelson, 1997.

De Mello, Anthony. *Awareness: The Perils and Opportunities of Reality.* New York: Doubleday, 1992

Dominian, Jack. *Dynamics of Marriage: Love, Sex, and Growth from a Christian Perspective.* Mystic CT: Twenty-Third Publications, 1993.

Dyckman, Katherine; Mary Garvin, and Elizabeth Liebert. *The Spiritual Exercises Reclaimed: uncovering Liberating Possibilities for Women.* New York: Paulist Press, 2001.

Delio, Ilio. *The Unbearable Wholeness of Being, God, Evolution and the Power of Love.* New York, Orbis Press, 2013.

English, John. *Spiritual Freedom.* Guelph, Ontario: Loyola House, 1987.

Fleming, David L. SJ. *Draw Me into Your Friendship: The Spiritual Exercises, Literal Translation & A Contemporary Reading.* St. Louis: The Institute of Jesuit Sources. 1996.

_____. *What is Ignatian Spirituality?* Chicago: Loyola Press, 2008.

Gaillardetz, Richard R. *A Daring Promise: A Spirituality of Christian Marriage.* Liguori, MO: Liguori/Triumph, 2007.

Garrido, Ann M. *Redeeming Conflict: 12 Habits for Christian Leaders.* Notre Dame, IN: Ave Maria Press, 2016

Gottman, John. *Why Marriages Succeed or Fail and How You Can Make Yours Last.* New York: Simon & Schuster, 1994.

_____. *The Seven Principles for Making Marriage Work.* New York: Three Rivers Press, 2000.

Harter, Michael SJ. (ed.), *Hearts on Fire.* St. Louis: The Institute of Jesuit Sources, 1993.

Kasper, Walter Cardinal. *The Gospel of the Family.* New York: Paulist Press, 2014.

Keating, Thomas. *The Human Condition. Contemplation and Transformation.* New York: Paulist Press, 1999.

Kritsberg, Wayne. *The Adult Children of Alcoholics Syndrome*. New York: Bantam Books, 1985.

Law, Maureen Rogers and Lanny Law. *Marriage Isn't Always Easy*. Notre Dame, IN: Sorin Books 2002.

Lawler, Michael. *Time, Sex and Money, the First 5 years of Marriage*. Omaha: Creighton University, Center for Marriage and Family, 2000.

Loyola, Ignatius. *A Pilgrim's Testament. The Memoirs of St. Ignatius of Loyola. Transcribed by Luis Goncalves de Camara*. St. Louis, Institute of Jesuit Sources, 1995.

Manney, Jim. *A Simple Life-Changing prayer: Discovering the Power of St. Ignatius Loyola's Examen*. Chicago: Loyola Press, 2011.

_____. *God Finds Us. An Experience of the Spiritual Exercises of St. Ignatius Loyola*. Chicago: Loyola Press, 2013.

Markman, Howard J., Scott M. Stanley, and Susan L. Blumberg. *Fighting for Your Marriage*. Greenwood Village, CO: PREP Educational Products, Inc. 1996.

Martin, James, SJ. *The Jesuit Guide to (Almost) Everything*. New York: HarperCollins Publishers, 2010.

_____. *Becoming Who You Are*. Mahwah, NJ: HiddenSpring, 2006.

May, Gerald G. MD. *The Awakened Heart: Opening Yourself to the Love You Need*. New York: HarperCollins Publishers, 1993.

Merrill, Nan C. *Psalms for Praying: An Invitation to Wholeness*. New York: Continuum, 2002.

Modras, Ronald. *Ignatian Humanism*. Chicago: Loyola Press, 2004.

Moore, Thomas. *Soul Mates, Honoring the Mysteries of Love and Relationship*. New York: HarperCollins, 1994.

_____. *The Soul of Sex, Cultivating Life as an Act of Love*. New York: Harper Perennial, 1999.

Muldoon, Tim and Sue. *Six Sacred Rules for Families*. Notre Dame, IN: Ava Maria Press, 2013.

_____. *The Discerning Parent: An Ignatian Guide to Raising Your Teenager*. Notre Dame, IN: Ave Maria Press, 2017.

Muldoon, Tim. *Longing to Love*. Chicago: Loyola Press, 2010.

_____. *Ignatian Workout for Lent 40 Days of Prayer, Reflection, and Action*. Chicago: Loyola Press, 2013.

_____. *The Ignatian Workout: Daily Spiritual Exercises for a Healthy Faith*. Chicago: Loyola Press, 2004.

Myers, Isabel Briggs and Peter Myers. *Gifts Differing: Understanding Personality Types*. Palo Alto: Davies-Black, 1980.

Nouwen, Henri J. M. *The Return of the Prodigal Son*. New York: Doubleday, 1992.

O' Brien, Kevin SJ. *The Ignatius Adventure. Experiencing the Spiritual Exercises of St. Ignatius in Daily Life*. Chicago: Loyola Press 2011.

O'Malley, William J. *Connecting with God: Prayers for Those Who Have Yet to Find the Words*. Maryknoll, NY: Orbis Books, 2013.

Pedersen, Mary Jo. *For Better, For Worse, For God*. Chicago: Loyola Press, 2008.

Pope Francis. *The Joy of the Gospel: Evangellii Gaudium*. Washington, DC: USCCB, 2013.

_____. *The Joy of Love: Amoris Laetitia*. Washington, DC: USCCB, 2016.

Pope John Paul II. *The Role of Christian Family in the Modern World: Familiaris Consortio*. Boston: The Daughters of St. Paul, 1981.

Pramuk, Christopher. *At Play in Creation: Merton's Awakening to the Feminine Divine*. Collegeville: Liturgical Press, 2015.

Savary, Louis. *The New Spiritual Exercises. In the Spirit of Pierre Teilhard de Chardin*. New York: Paulist Press. 2010.

Schillebeeckx, Edward. *Marriage, Human Reality and Saving Mystery*. New York: Sheed and Ward, 1965.

Sheldrake, Philip. *Befriending Our Desires*. Ottawa: Novalis, 2001.

Silf, Margaret, *Inner Compass: An Invitation to Ignatian Spirituality*. Chicago: Loyola Press, 1999.

Smith, Carol Ann and Merz, Eugene F. Moment by Moment: *A Retreat in Everyday Life*. Notre Dame, IN: Ava Maria Press, 2000.

Tetlow, Joseph A. SJ, *Choosing Christ in the World*. St. Louis: The Institute of Jesuit Sources, 1989.

Sparough, J. Michael, SJ, Manney, Jim, Hipskind, Tim, SJ. *What's Your Decision?: How to Make Choices with Confidence and Clarity*. Chicago: Loyola Press, 2010.

Traub, George W. SJ. *An Ignatian Spiritual Reader*. Chicago: Loyola Press, 2008.

Westley, Dick. *Redemptive Intimacy: A New Perspective for the Journey to Adult Faith*. Mystic, CT: Twenty-Third Publications, 1981.

Zimmerman, Jeffrey, Elizabeth Thayer. *Adult Children of Divorce*. Oakland, CA: New Harbinger Publications, 2003.

IX
Glossary of Ignatian Terms

18th Annotation: (Lightworks) A shorter version of the Spiritual Exercises for individuals who may not be available to do the 19th Annotation, which covers all the Spiritual Exercises. Key elements of the Spiritual Exercises are presented for prayer and reflection.

19th Annotation Retreat [19] (Retreat in Daily Living): A retreat carried out in daily life in the face of normal occupations and living conditions for the extent of the whole retreat. The retreatant should determine, along with the director, the amount of time each day for prayer so that the director can divide up the matter accordingly.

A.M.D.G. Ad Majoren Dei Gloriam (Latin) For the greater glory of God. Motto of the Jesuits.

Christian Life Community: The Christian Life Community (CLC) is an international association of lay Christians who have adopted an Ignatian model of spiritual life. Each Community lives out their Ignatian vocation in their own culture. The Community is present in almost 60 countries. Website: www.clc-usa.org

Consolation [316]: This term describes our interior life:

   a)   when we find ourselves so on fire with the love of God that we can
        freely give ourselves to God;

b) when we are saddened for our infidelity to God but at the same time thankful to know God as our Savior;

c) when we find our life of faith, hope, and love so strengthened and emboldened any increase in faith, hope, or love that the joy of serving God is foremost in our life.

Contemplation (Ignatian): Contemplation is more about feeling than thinking. Contemplation often stirs the emotions and enkindles deep desires. In contemplation, we rely on our imaginations to place ourselves in a setting from the Gospels or in a scene proposed by Ignatius. We pray the scriptures. We do not study it.

Discernment: A process for making choices in a context of faith, when the option is between or among several possible courses of action, all of which are potentially good.

Desolation [317]: This term describes our interior life:

a) when we find ourselves enmeshed in a certain turmoil of spirit or feel ourselves weighed down by a heavy darkness or weight;

b) when we experience a decrease of faith or hope or love in the distaste for prayer or for any spiritual activity and we know a certain restlessness or tepidity in our carrying on in the service of God;

c) when we experience just the opposite effect of what has been described as spiritual consolation.

Examen or Examen of Consciousness: Examen is a simple prayer directed toward developing an awareness of the ways God is present to one today. The Examen is primarily a time of prayer; it is a "being with God." It focuses on one's consciousness of God, not necessarily one's conscience regarding sins and mistakes. Ignatius considered the Examen the most important prayer.

Finding God in all things: Ignatian Spirituality is summed up in this phrase. It invites a person to find God in every circumstance of life; it implies that God is everywhere.

Guide: A person trained in discernment and the Spiritual Exercises who can guide another person to discover how God is working in his/her life.

Ignatius of Loyola (1491–1556): A Basque who was raised in the court of Ferdinand and Isabella. While defending the fortress town of Pamplona, he was injured when a cannonball shattered his leg. In his long recovery, Ignatius read the lives of the saints and was inspired to go to the Holy Land, where he hoped to dedicate his life "converting the unbelievers." Enroute to the Holy Land, he spent a year in Manresa, Spain, in prayer and reflection and where he wrote notes for his Spiritual Exercises. Returning from his brief stay in the Holy Land, Ignatius returned to Europe and began his formal schooling at the University of Paris. While there, he met Francis Xavier and Peter Faber, as well as Nicholas Bobadilla, Alfonso Salmeron, and Diego Lainez. After graduation, these men came together to form an apostolic community that became the Society of Jesus.

Incarnation: A mystery of faith that celebrates the Word of God (Jesus Christ) becoming man and dwelling among us.

Inordinate attachments: Ignatius uses this term to remind us that in order to move toward spiritual freedom and a deeper relationship with God we must be open to letting go of those things, people, attitudes, desires, and habits that would keep us from totally giving ourselves over to God.

Just Faith Groups: Just Faith Ministries provides programs that transform people and expand their commitment to social ministry. Through these life-changing opportunities, members of a church or parish can study, explore and experience Christ's call to care for the poor and vulnerable in a lively, challenging, multifaceted process in the context of a small faith community. Website: www.justfaith.org.

Magis (Latin for the more): A key Jesuit/Ignatian phrase that motivates a person to do and be "more" in one's work and service.

Meditation: We use our minds in meditation. We ponder the basic principles that guide our life. We pray over words, images, and ideas.

Principle of Indifference [23]: Principle of Indifference means that we do not prefer or choose one thing or another on their own merits. We should not prefer health to sickness, riches to poverty, honor to dishonor, a long life to a short life. We should desire and choose that which better leads to God's deepening life in us.

Spiritual Direction: Spiritual direction explores a deeper relationship with the spiritual aspect of being human. Simply put, spiritual direction is helping people tell their sacred stories every day. See Spiritual Directors International's website, www.sdiworld.org, for a directory of spiritual directors.

Spiritual Freedom: Freedom to choose that which brings one closer to God and to reject that which takes one away from God. A person gains this freedom when she or he is freed from fears and inordinate attachments that limit choice.

Spiritual Exercises: An organized series of Spiritual Exercises put together by Ignatius of Loyola out of his own personal spiritual experience and that of others to whom he listened. Ignatius put all of this down in the book of the Spiritual Exercises to create a handbook to help the guide who coaches a person engaged in "making the exercises."

X
Resources

There are numerous resources for both healthy marriage skills and Ignatian Spirituality that you may want to explore. The ones listed below are resources that we have found very helpful. Also, peruse the Bibliography for books that may pique your interest.

Specific books on Ignatian Spirituality that are excellent resources:

The Ignatian Tradition. Spirituality in History. Eileen Burke-Sullivan, Kevin Burke, SJ, and Phyllis Zagano, Series Editor. Collegeville MN: Liturgical Press, 2009.

The Spiritual Exercises Reclaimed: Uncovering Liberating Possibilities for Women. K. Dyckman, M. Garvin, E. Liebert. New York: Paulist Press, 2001.

A Simple Life-Changing Prayer, Discovering the Power of St. Ignatius Loyola's Examen. Jim Manney, Chicago: Loyola Press. 2011.

The Jesuit Guide to (Almost) Everything, A Spirituality for Real Life. James Martin, SJ, New York: HarperCollins, 2001.

The Ignatian Adventure, Experiencing the Spiritual Exercises of Saint Ignatius in Daily Life. Kevin O'Brien, SJ, Chicago: Loyola Press, 2011.

Inner Compass: An Invitation to Ignatian Spirituality. Margaret Silf, Chicago: Loyola Press, 1999.

Marriage and Family Spirituality:

Claiming Our Deepest Desires, the Power of an Intimate Marriage. Bridget Brennan and Jerome Shen, Collegeville, MN: Liturgical Press, 2004.

M. Bridget Brennan and Jerome L. Shen

Redeeming Conflict, 12 Habits for Christian Leaders. Ann Garrido, Notre
    Dame. IN: Ave Maria Press, 2016. Written for Christian leaders but
    also excellent information for couples in conflict.
Six Sacred Rules for Families, A Spirituality for the Family. Tim and Sue
    Muldoon, Notre Dame, IN: Ave Maria Press, 2013.

Healthy Marriage Skills:

The Seven Principles for Making Marriage Work, John Gottman, New York:
    Three Rivers Press (a division of Random House). 1999.
Five Love Languages, How to Express Heartfelt Commitment to Your Mate.
    Gary Chapman., Chicago: Northfield Publishing 2004 (edition).

Websites and Blogs:

USCCB
www.foryourmarriage.org

The Society of Jesus in the U.S.
www.jesuit.org

Ignatian Spirituality
http://ignatianspirituality.com

Creighton University Online 34-week Retreat for Everyday Life
http://onlineministries.creighton.edu/CollaborativeMinsistry/cmo-retreat

Xavier University — Jesuit Resource
http://xavier.edu/jesuitresources/

Sacred Space Daily Meditations from the Irish Jesuits
http://sacredspace.ie/

Prayer Windows: Ignatian Prayer Using Art
http://www.prayerwindows.com

Loyal Institute, Orange, Calif.
www.LoyolaInstitute.org

Ignatian Spirituality Center, Santa Clara University.
www.scu.edu

Ignatian Spirituality Center, Seattle University.
www.Ignatiancenter.org

Ignatian Spirituality Project (ISP) Chicago.
www.IgnatianSpiritualityProject.org

Ignatian Spiritual Exercises for the Corporate Person (ISECP).
http://isecp.org/

Christian Life Cummunities
US www.clc-usa.org   **International** www.cvx-clc.net

Finding the Divine
www.findingthedivine.org

www.bustedhalo.org

www.Godinallthings.org

Do you want to know more about "what makes you tick" or "what makes your spouse tick"? Online Personality inventories can be found at:

www.Keirsey.com and www.humanmetrics.com
www.myers-brigg personality type indicator (the original inventory)
www.16personalities.com (free inventory online)

Volunteer Opportunities:

Jesuit Volunteer Corps: Dare to Change, Ages 21–35
Serve for one-year. jesuitvolunteers.org

Ignatian Volunteer Corps Experience Making a Difference
For women and men 50 years or older. Serve two days a week, 10 months per year. www.ivcusa.org

Brief Biography

M. Bridget Brennan has a B. A. in Education and Sociology and a M. A. in Human Relations as well as a M. A. in Religious Studies. She is a Certified Family Life Educator, Relationship Skills Coach, master level, and a Marriage Preparation Educator. She is also trained in the PREP and PAIRS programs.

Jerome L. Shen has a Ph. D. in chemistry. Jerry was the Director of Research for Ralston-Purina and Assistant Professor at Southern Illinois University at Edwardsville. Jerry has also been trained in PREP and PAIRS, and other relationship programs.

Jerry and Bridget have presented workshops on *Living Ignatian Spirituality in Marriage* at several Ignatian Conferences at St. Louis University.

Bridget and Jerry have traveled throughout the US presenting retreats for couples; workshops at national conferences: Smart Marriages; NACFLM; Missouri Social Services; US Adm. of Children and Families; and many more regional conferences and programs at parishes and spirituality centers.

We have developed and directed a marriage preparation seminar for first time and second time marriages. Over the 18 years, we have prepared over 5,000 couples for marriage.

In our work, Jerry tends to seek the ideal and Bridget keeps us grounded with the practical. Together, we can seek ideals that are attainable in our practical reality.

This book and our first book - *Claiming our Deepest Desires: The Power of an Intimate Marriage* - came from our experience. We write this second book in gratitude to God and to those who have helped and enriched our marriage and spiritual journey.